Competitive Irish Dance

Competitive Irish Dance
Art, Sport, Duty

Frank Hall

MACATER
P R E S S

Macater Press
PO Box 44305
Madison, Wisconsin 53744

www.macaterpress.com

Printed in the United States of America

Hall, Frank
Competitive Irish dance: art, sport, duty
ISBN 978-0-9814924-2-1
Library of Congress Control Number: 2008931223

Cover design: Flying Fish Graphics
Cover photo: Emily Sanderson, Claddagh Dance Company, California. Photo by Tim Allen.

For Brendan and Elena

Table of Contents

Illustrations

Preface

How on earth did Irish dancing come to take the form it has, both in body movement and as a recognized theatrical genre? In the most general sense, this is the question I shall attempt to answer. When this study began, however, Irish dancing was not so well known. The original question motivating this study was: what happens when an aesthetic form is put into a competitive frame? What happens to an art form that is practiced as a sport? And quite honestly, I wanted to know why the Irish dancers I saw were so amazingly dexterous with their feet while so frozen above the waist. At a more fundamental level, I wanted to explore the question of how movement has meaning and significance.

This book is aimed at two different groups of readers—those with curiosity and interest in Irish dancing, and students of dance and human movement systems. It is an extended argument about the study of dancing, and a description of a fascinating form of dance that is both a marvelous cultural achievement and a solid global theatrical presence. Thus arguments about the anthropology of dance (and human movement systems in general) are interspersed with descriptions and elucidations of Irish dancing itself—its form, its history, its modes of practice. As a courtesy to non-specialist readers, I have relegated most of the technical discussions to the footnotes and to the appendix.

Each chapter is, in effect, its own short treatise. Thus the chapters of this book can be read in any order. The Introduction lays out the themes and topics developed throughout—authority, authenticity, and control. In Chapter One I start with the posture of Irish dancing because it is the topic about which I am asked most often. An exploration of posture also involves the topics of nationalist history and competitive practice that follow in Chapters Two and Three. Chapter Four takes a very different perspective— the dance class—where movement and meaning are inseparably learned as a practice. Chapter Five pursues this topic into the area of creativity and questions of identity. I conclude in Chapter Six with a discussion of the development of Irish dance stage shows from and through *Riverdance*.

᠉

I first saw Irish dancing at a fiddlers' gathering in Battleground, Indiana, 1973. It was a young 14-year-old Michael Flatley and his brother Patrick who danced a duet onstage accompanied by several Chicago musicians. One of these musicians was Kevin Henry who, after the Flatleys had danced, demonstrated the old-style (seán nos) step dancing. Irish dancing made an impression on me then and repeatedly whenever I saw it performed. It further raised my curiosity when I found it was taught in "dance schools" and mainly performed in competitions. Very organized, I thought, for a folk dance.

The fieldwork for this study was begun in 1987 in the United States and mainly pursued in Ireland during 1988 and 1991, though informed by other fieldwork also in Ireland in 1999 and 2003. Though I met and visited teachers from many locations, the bulk of the research took place in Galway, Limerick, and Dublin, working with teachers from five different schools of Irish dancing. I was, I think, a bit of a curiosity to my hosts, yet I was always treated with great kindness and warmth. Celine Hession and Máirín Ní Ruairc-Tuathaigh especially put up with an awful lot of questions and struggled to make some use of my presence in their classes.

From the start I was more interested in the form of Irish dancing than in the social relations around it. However, my perspective shifted when looking at the various social roles involved in the schools and competitions. It became apparent to me that, though there are many different and interesting personalities involved in the dancing, they were all influenced more or less deeply by the pressures inherent in the competitive process. While one could make an analysis of how various personalities respond to competition, I chose instead to focus on the pressures that seemingly no one can escape. Consequently I have often changed or omitted names to keep the focus on social pressures that stem from the cultural practice rather than on the individuals and their unique responses to them.

Irish dancing is a huge topic and invites many kinds of study. In no way is this book meant to be a complete treatment of the subject. I have explored the form through a focus on specific issues and questions. Much remains to be done especially in terms of the economic and social dimensions of Irish dance in relationship to issues of class, nationalism, transnationalism, ethnicity, and globalism. But if this work proves useful to others looking at this dance practice or other dance forms in general, I will be delighted.

Acknowledgments

When I came to Ireland to begin this study in 1991, I didn't see it as an affair of the heart. In June of that year I was diagnosed with constrictive pericarditis and underwent open heart surgery at the Mater in Dublin. Life changed. I owe a great debt to my partner at the time, Mary Beth Roska, and to friends back home in Bloomington, Indiana who rallied to support me and to raise money for my continued research. In particular I am grateful to James Chiplis, Margie Van Auken, Cindy Levindofske, and Abby Ladin, as well as The Monks and the whole Bloomington Old-Time Music and Dance community. In Ireland I enjoyed the kindness and camaraderie of Claire Carré, Mike and Sue Fahy, Cath Taylor, Cepta Byrne, Johnny Moynihan, the set dancers at Monroe's, and the many dance and musician friends in both Ireland and the U.S. Though I returned to Indiana for a decade, I eventually wandered back to Ireland for a longer stay. As I finished the intellectual work I had started and then moved on to other fields of endeavor, I began to recognize the gifts of cooperation, support, engagement, and indulgence that made the original study possible for the blessings they were and are.

I am humbled by the generosity of my Irish dancing consultants including, but by no means limited to: Celine Hession, Christina Howard, Máirín Ní Tuathaigh, Jack O'Brian, Orfhlaith Ní Bhriain, John Cullinane, Paul Moran, Gemma Carney, Tony Ryan, Marie Duffy, Gearóid ÓTuathaigh, Marie Philbin, Seamus MacConuladh, Peggy McTeggart, John Timm, Ann Richens, Mary McGing, and the many dancers, adjudicators, teachers, parents, and commission members who indulged my endless questions.

For their intellectual engagement and collegial support, I thank Anya Royce, Richard Bauman, Henry Glassie, Carol Greenhouse, Joelle Bahloul, Drid Williams, Brenda Farnell, Charles Varella, Bridget Edwards, and Desi Wilkinson. Mícheál Ó Súilleabháin and Catherine Foley extended much appreciated professional courtesies, opportunities, and academic support many times over the years of this project and since.

Several people helped immensely in bringing this book to fruition. I thank Morris Meyer for lighting a fire under me to finish the work. Paula Níc Cionnaith provided essential translations of early Commission meeting minutes as well as great perspective as dancer and Irish speaker. Sarah Ryterband read the manuscript countless times in the early stages and offered valuable advice as a non-specialist. I appreciate her many forms of assistance and support over the years. Didi Delap edited a late version, and Stuart Smyth came to my rescue with photography needed to replace lost or inadequate fieldwork photos. For closeness and understanding in the final stages and for a rich musical life I thank my partner, Lena, and recognize the enriching community of music lovers and players in the Kinvara area.

Introduction

Rachael Ann is taking the stage. The room falls silent. She is somehow very present, centered on the stage, centered in the room, poised, prepared. The musician starts the tune, "The Three Sea Captains." Now she leaps, taps, steps, and the flow of rhythm begins.

Like many of the others she is beautiful and graceful, tense and aggressive—a combination of features that fits Irish dancing and made me love it (in an uneasy sort of way) from the first time I saw it. The upper half of the body is held still, sometimes (perhaps inadvertently) rigid. Meanwhile the legs and feet work in either propellant aerial gymnastics or forceful audible rhythms to create a dynamic neither contradicted nor balanced but contrasted with the torso, chest, arms, and head. It is as if the restraint of the upper half of the dancing body has resulted in movement with a vengeance in the lower half. This combination of restriction and expression gives the form a remarkable power.

Eleven months of looking at competitive Irish dancing through the lens of anthropology has brought me here, to the Munster Oireachtas, the last of the four provincial championships in Ireland for the year. I stand at the back of the hall packed among teachers and mothers, grandmothers, cousins, and uncles. Not a dancer's relative, I look for some way to identify, someone to pull for, a way to belong and transform this mere activity into drama. I have been standing too long (my feet feel like lead weights), watching too long, as dancer after dancer executes her routine, all seemingly the same to the casual observer. I had grown casual. I desired now to enter the illusion in which the performance is all-important, as it was to Rachael Ann.

An observer, an academic, an outsider, how can I know the hope, the dread, the tension, the expectations that accompany a dancer onstage? Above the hours—no, weeks, years—of grueling work on the part of the dancer, there is the parental investment: costumes, lessons, countless lifts to and fro, arrangements, the lesser competitions, the accommodations many and myriad that result in the dancer's entrance onstage. For the dancer and everyone connected with her, the provincial championships either end the year in defeat or open the door to the highest level of contest, the Oireachtas Rince na Cruinne—the World Championships.

Rachael is my connection. She glides across the stage, now leaps, kicks, stamps, turns, ankles twisting and rotating, a ripple of beats and POW— another stamp. Can she win? The World Championship this year will be held in Limerick, near her hometown. Rachael Ann danced in it last year. She did not place highly, but she danced well, a respectable showing where it is an honor to compete at all. Could she go to the Worlds as the Munster champion?

Rachael Ann is Maureen's student. Three years ago I phoned Maureen, interested in doing research on Irish dancing; could I talk to her? "Of course." When I came to Limerick I called again. She wanted to know where I was. I gave her the name of the B & B I had just checked into. "Stupid eejit!" she said. "Have you paid yet?" "No." I walked out under a barrage of accusations from the owner: what a typical American I was, taking advantage. Maureen picked me up and I stayed with her family. That evening after dance class, Maureen asked which dancers I liked. I had been impressed by Michael. I mentioned also Rachael Ann. "Yes," said Maureen, "she wins a lot."

I hold still now as Rachael Ann dances. My eyes zoom in on her feet. What's that? A slip. Slight, but noticeable. A sole sliding on the floor, a momentary loss of grip. Her feet continue the step combination, but only for another moment: it takes time for her to register that she has slipped, so intense is her concentration. But now she stops.

I stop. We stop. The audience hung in a space out of time, the ground pulled out from under us all. The music continues. But Rachael Ann is walking now, almost wandering, dazed, back and around to her starting point. We are still suspended between our expectations and our realizations. What will she do? Will she start again? What will they do—the musician, the officials? Can she start again? The music approaches the end of the phrase and she points her toe in preparation. She leaps into her first step. The music stops.

Of course. It was the end of the tune. It was not up to the musician to make a decision to continue, to play over again, a second chance for Rachael Ann where others got only one. Rachael Ann smiles. She nods and slightly waves her hand as if to say, "Yes, I understand. It's OK." She walks off the stage composed, certainly not yet thinking of all the implications. The end of her dance-year's trajectory.

Maureen's daughter, also a teacher, runs across the room to the side of the stage where Rachael Ann descends. Orla will be the first to talk to her. And what will she say? We remain suspended. The next dancer begins. A small crowd now encloses Rachael. They will keep her from lonely thoughts. More dancers come and go. Is this the end of the year for Rachael Ann? The last dancer leaves the stage. An official approaches the adjudicators seated on tables above the level of mere spectators. He shuttles back and forth between them. He approaches the microphone. "Could we have Number Five back to dance her set again please?"

Applause. Relief. Somehow it doesn't seem fair to end her year with a slip. Number Five takes the stage again. But I wonder, won't someone complain that she got a second chance? How will the officials defend their decision? These competitions bring out all possible arguments on both sides of any decision that affects the qualification for the Worlds of one dancer over another. Rachael Ann has begun to dance. Her dancing is not as strong as some in producing the sound, but she is accurate and looks the part. *"Best legs in Irish dancing!" Maureen once said to me.* But now she stops in mid-step. Her concentration is broken. No physical slip this time. She raises her hand to her forehead, looks puzzled. Where has that step gone? It was well in her feet before.

This time we all know it's over. When Rachael Ann descends the stage, her people are there to take her in their arms. They let her cry and perhaps tell her not to dwell on it; it's not the end of the world, ironic now as that might sound. But she is broken for the moment. Broken as anyone would be. I approach Maureen after a while. I will see Michael dance, but then I must go. I will say my goodbyes now. "It has not been a good week for us," she says.

This last episode only caps what has been a number of disappointments for her school. The screams of joy that accompany announced results signify only the winners and those who place. These are the few. The ranks of the disappointed are many. One does not hear their silence and only rarely hears grumbles. One could look for reasons: that costume is too old; this adjudicator never liked us—the contamination of pure dance evaluation with economics and politics. Within a school, a few successes make the greater number of disappointments bearable, maybe eclipses them altogether. But when the successes don't come, and slips or breaks in concentration steal the expected, then disappointments weigh heavily. Now my identification with Rachael Ann's performance through Maureen's help and friendship has led me deeper into a network of feelings and knowings. The disappointment is real. The week has not been good to Maureen and her school.

"But what harm?" she says. I nod. What harm indeed? Only broken confidence, shattered expectations, embarrassment. Only feelings. They mend. In fact, it is the low that makes the high possible. Any mystic knows that.

I'm saying my goodbye now and Rachael Ann walks by. Maureen reaches out and grabs her arm. "Your face is far too beautiful to be spoiled with tears." Her voice, mock-scolding in tone, is tinged with pathos and full in its warmth. Rachael Ann wipes her cheek in the face of this wisdom.

I watch Michael dance, and he dances well. Surely a winner. I'll leave now. I don't need to know where Michael places just at the moment. I'll slip out of the hall, back home to Galway, then home to Indiana. It is hard to tell what is won and what is lost at these contests.[1]
Ennis, 1991

❧

Irish dancing is art made sport. The contest pits the bodily expressiveness of one dancer against others. One theme of that expression, inherent in the contest, is that Irishness itself is represented in body movement. The winner is not just the best dancer but the best *Irish* dancer. These two features—competition and nationalism—have shaped the development of the form, the actual use of the body, and the structure of experiences enmeshed in the world of Irish dancing.

Irish dancing is many things: a social network, a cultural form, an expressive practice, an individual achievement, a family investment, a ritual drama, a national symbol, an endless series of entertaining events, and one of the most extraordinary and highly developed dance forms in the contemporary world—a classical tradition now in its own right. Individual experiences of Irish dancing must be as many and as varied as the participants, their talents, and their social positions. Nevertheless, the claim to represent nationality together with the competitive framework are two facts shaping all performances of Irish dance (even *Riverdance* and other theatrical presentations of Irish dancing) because they shape the movement itself.

In 1994, at the Eurovision Song Contest, Irish step-dancing leapt onto the world stage of popular culture via *Riverdance.* Originally a between-acts interlude, it proved so popular that it was expanded into a full-length theatrical production which in turn has spawned numerous break-away productions and imitators. *Lord of the Dance* took the dancing to hyperbolic theatrical extremes with smoke, fire, lights, music collapsed to a soundtrack, and female dancers who remove their skirts in competition over the oiled-up and leathered male star, the "lord" himself.

These developments of Irish dancing have produced mixed reactions among observers and participants, myself included. One undoubted effect is that Irish dancing is no longer quite the parochial activity that it was, something to be seen only rarely outside of the competitions.[2] Suddenly everyone knows Irish dancing. The regiments of look-alike dancers in line beating out that thunder have become an icon. It has been both used and parodied in TV sitcoms and advertisements. The world is aware of the form, its power, subtlety, and impressive technique. This awareness itself is a significant change.

There is also significant continuity. When dancers and teachers of Irish dancing first looked at the oiled Michael Flatley (original star of both *Riverdance* and *Lord of the Dance*) posing, strutting, and flourishing his arms, they may have said, "That's not Irish dancing." Meanwhile, much of the audience was discovering "Irish dancing." Flatley was moving in and out of the aesthetic standards of Irish dancing, incorporating elements from other forms, notably tap and flamenco. He also moved in and out of the corps of dancers who were doing solid and recognizable Irish dancing. Thus for the Irish dance cognoscenti the question of identity was significant: Is this Irish dancing? Is this *now* Irish dancing? Is this the new standard? Should this *be* the new standard? However, these are not unfamiliar questions in the practice of competitive Irish step-dancing itself.

The theatrical productions recapitulate the same issues enacted in competitive dancing, though they do so more dramatically and in a new arena. These issues are authenticity, authority, and control. They involve the morality of expressive body movement, tradition in art forms, national and ethnic identity, and the contradictions of competition and cooperation. These are the themes explored in this book. They are connected to the history of Irish dancing, to the contemporary practice in dancing schools, dancing contests, dance theatre, and to the form of the movement itself.

Authority, authenticity, and control of culture are issues that resonate far beyond the contests and theatrical shows. Perhaps audiences for Irish dance theatre appreciate at some visceral level the relevance of these themes embodied in the form of dancing itself where control is manifest in both bodily discipline and rhythmic expression, where authority is evident in the high degree of technical achievement, and where authenticity remains a lively argument.[3] Behind this monumental theatrical achievement lies a nationalist history and a contemporary practice of aesthetic competition, both of which inform and result in the impressiveness of Irish dancing.

My own perspective on Irish dancing enters and participates in the issues I take as my main themes: authority, authenticity, and control. Each of these can be triangulated with the notion of Ireland and the activity we call "dancing."

Authority: Anthropology and Ireland
This book began as an anthropological and ethnographic treatise on Irish dancing. As such it fits into a particular academic discipline, tradition, and point-of-view on cultures and the societies that produce those cultures. The origin of anthropology is a search for answers to the question, "What is human?" Its methods—ethnography and comparison—recognize the importance of both difference and commonality between human groups. Ethnography focuses on a specific human group and asks the question: why do these people do what they do in the particular way that they do it? By carving up the vast human whole this way and comparing the various answers we get a purchase on the larger question of human identity, so we believe. The particular question that motivated me, as a dancer and musician myself, was "what happens when you put an expressive form, say dancing, into a competitive framework?"

This project is an ethnography of people who are in some sense ethnographing themselves in this activity. That is to say, they present and re-present themselves as a cultural group (ethnicity or nation) when they perform Irish dancing. It might be said that they literally embody the values they associate ideally with their identity as a national culture. As a sustained argument about what and how Irish dancing means, this book is focused squarely on the movement itself and the talk surrounding the movement. It assumes that to appreciate the richness of meaning it helps to understand the historical, cultural, and social context of the activity.

This ethnography is not a community study in the typical sense (based in a locality), a genre whose origins are often attributed to Arensberg and Kimball's work done in County Clare, Ireland in the 1930s.[4] This is a study of a form of movement, a cultural product, a collective representation produced by natives and by descendants of the Irish diaspora as well as others around the globe. Still, the study was carried out mostly in Ireland itself, in Galway, Limerick, Cork, and Dublin.

Although anthropological studies of Ireland have been based in specific locations, many authors have used their findings to represent Irish culture generally. *The Irish Countryman* (1937), which sounds like it should describe all Irish country people, was based on fieldwork done in just one county—Clare. It may be difficult for anthropologists to avoid using their data to generalize about larger populations. Some, like Henry Glassie, in *Passing the Time in Ballymenone* (1982), have managed to avoid the type of generalization that claims the work describes a "nation's folk," as Arensberg put it *(Irish Countryman* 15).

When one makes a study of Irish dancing, so called by the people who do it, one studies the process of generalization itself. Here people are representing themselves, but more than themselves, as individuals, saying (in both spoken and body languages) what Irishness is.[5] One is looking at the process of identity negotiation itself for an "imagined community," in Benedict Anderson's suggestive term for "nation" (in *Imagined Communities*).

What is Irish about Irish dancing? With this question we enter a mine-field, but one that is home to anthropology. What kind of claim to knowledge can any outsider make regarding another's cultural form? Can one avoid the coup of psycho-cultural projection—explaining someone else in terms of one's own hang-ups? To ask what is Irish about the activity is to raise the issue of authenticity. This question is integral to the practice of competitive solo step-dancing itself, as competitors vie for honors as the best Irish dancer. The standard criticism for any aspect of the practice, from a dance movement to a costume innovation, is: "That's not Irish dancing," or "That's not Irish." So what is Irish dancing? Can an anthropological point of view resolve what the Irish and Irish dancers themselves debate?

No. But it might be possible to outline points of the debate, main themes, and recurring issues as they arise from a history of the practice (Chapters One and Two), from the human drama engaged and prosecuted in competitions (Chapter Three), from the structure of the form of dancing itself as learned by children (Chapter Four), from the creative process of choreography for competitive dancing (Chapter Five), and from consideration of the changes wrought in the form as it moves from contest to theatre (Chapter Six). The practice of Irish dancing reveals an underlying logic of both aesthetic competition and nationalist symbology. Some of this logic is shared with competitions and living national symbols everywhere. The culturally specific, the "Irishness" of the activity, is an ongoing debate in the form and practice of the dancing. It is not susceptible to definition or reduction. Even though the form of dancing—its rules, grammar, structure—can be outlined, its meaning and significance continue to shift and change with time, place, and social context.

Authenticity: Ireland and Dancing

In 1988 I met an American anthropologist who had worked in Ireland. I told him I was hoping to do anthropological fieldwork there myself, that I wished to look at Irish dancing. "Oh, well," he quickly replied, "you know there are two kinds of Irish dancing: the fake kind done by little girls in gaudy dresses and the real stuff known only by a few old men here and there."

In folkloristic circles there is an aura of authenticity that surrounds the category of *sean-nós* (old-style) step-dancing. This is a form that has not been subjected to an institutionalized competitive context nor, until recently, taught in classes. It is a more informal practice, very much alive and recently undergoing a resurgence in interest. However, my own interest was in the questions: 1.) what happens to an expressive form when it is put into competition, made into sport; and 2.) what happens to an expressive form when it is specifically linked to national identity? So, apparently, I was interested in "the fake stuff." Authenticity of culture is a theme that captures many a modern soul, including anthropologists and Irish dancers, even when they think they stand (or dance) outside these questions.

There is a story about Pablo Picasso—I don't remember where I heard it. He was going through a collection of paintings in order to identify authentic Picassos and fakes. His assistant showed him a particular piece that Picasso identified as a forgery. "But, Maestro," said the assistant, "Don't you remember this piece? I was here when you painted it." "Do you think that I cannot fake a Picasso?" was his reply. With this in mind, I take the approach that what is real and what is fake depends on perspective, context, and the purpose of the distinction.

Hervé Varenne, in "Confusion of Signs," has written about the tendency of Dubliners to direct anyone interested in Irish culture to the west coast of Ireland, toward the Gaeltachtaí, the Irish-speaking areas. Varenne made it his business to stay in a Dublin suburb and study Irish culture there, paying attention to, among other things, that part of the culture that constrains the urban Irish to look west to see themselves, so to speak. "The real Ireland" is hidden, ever-receding into the mists of a Celtic past, or disappearing with the Irish language on parts of the west coast, or dying with the few older men who remember the old step-dancing.

The anthropologist to whom I spoke in 1988, who labeled competitive dancing "fake," wanted to see authentic dancing as inheritance only, not creation or invention. Many people who have studied human movement tend also to want to see the human body as beyond the reach of mindfulness. But the facts are that people learn, create, and select ways of moving, acting, dancing. Irish dancers create and select with the materials of their inheritance to express values, both inherited and changing, through movement. They do so, however, within certain limitations, two of which are the context of competition and the politics of nationalism. Even though *Riverdance* has expanded the context of Irish dancing, the dancers who perform in this and other Irish dance theatre have learned their art form and technique through competition, in schools authenticated by nationalist organizations that are now international in membership.

In calling my subject matter "Irish dancing," I am following a nationalist typology of dancing in Ireland [Fig. 1]. I focus here on the modern competitive solo step-dancing--associated in this typology with a social dance form called "céilí" which is often performed in competition as well, though not exclusively. This may be seen as a tendentious labeling, especially for an anthropologist. It is a constructed term.[6] I can only say that I am not interested in answering questions as to which are "real" and "fake" forms, as if such categories exist outside someone's particular point of view. I take this typology from consultants, mainly dancers themselves, and accept that this is how they see it. Not everyone agrees. The shifting category in the middle, for example, is seen by some people as being every bit as Irish (and more, as with the anthropologist above) than the modern competitive step-dancing.

Sean-nós (old-style) refers to step-dancing which is not performed in the modern contest setting, though it may be informally competitive.[7] In the early 1990s it had been performed by mostly older dancers, however younger dancers have taken an interest in the form and it is now being taught in classes and workshops. In 1991 I saw it in only a few places such as Connemara, north Kerry, and Rathcairn, Co. Meath.[8] It differs from the modern step-dancing in form, especially in that there appears to be a much wider variation in posture, use of arms, hands, head, etc. Often the point is to make rhythms on the floor, but special shoes are not necessarily worn. This form of dance is not so much purposely excluded from the category "Irish dancing" as it appears to have simply been left behind, ig-

1. Nationalist Taxonomy of Dancing in Ireland, showing shifting placement of sean-nós (old-style) step-dancing and sets of quadrilles in the center (gray area) of a dichotomous assumption of nationalist identity (Irish/Other).

nored, or relegated to a past relevance by the practitioners of the modern competitive form.

The sets are another story. Nationalist thought more purposely excluded these from "Irish dancing" based on their foreign origin. While it is most likely true that quadrilles were introduced to Ireland by French- or English-trained dancing masters, the form as it was practiced in the Irish countryside in the nineteenth and early twentieth centuries had certainly undergone transformations that could only be described as Irish. As performed today, the two features that most readily distinguish the sets as local (Irish) in form and sensibility are the music and the basic steps. [9] The latter includes the practice of making rhythms with the feet using step patterns that are distinctively Irish.[10] While in musical and aesthetic qualities the sets are native to Ireland, in name they make no claim to represent Irishness in the way that competitive "Irish dancing" does.

We might say that the sets and sean-nós dancing have not been burdened with the task of representing Irishness, while competitive solo stepdancing has. Dancers obviously need not think about this, especially in the contest setting: they simply perform, execute the technique and choreography as well as possible, and await the evaluation of the judges. Representation of Irishness is built into the history and label of the dancing.

Control: Anthropology and Dancing

Writing about dancing carries its own burden of representation. The technique and key to control is to be found in the theory, methodology, and overall discipline informing the approach. It is only fair to introduce the theoretical approach so one can know what kind of control is being attempted. I have put this discussion, a look behind the scenes so to speak, in an Appendix. Here in the main text I continue my focus on how dancers control their bodies, their postures, their movements, as well as how larger organizations attempt to control the development of Irish dancing.

The single most obvious token of the theme of control in Irish dancing is the dancing posture itself. I begin with the posture, considering it a puzzle or riddle, the solution of which will lead us on to larger issues in the practice of Irish dancing (nationalism and competition), back to the level of the body language itself (learning and creativity), and the creation of new genres of Irish dancing in the theatrical shows spawned by *Riverdance*.

CHAPTER ONE

Posture in Irish Dancing

> The dancing master was a very strict disciplinarian. Everything
> had to be dead spot on. When you started dancing, you were
> put in the corner with two little pieces of timber under your
> heels, because that was the height your heels had to be off the
> floor. You danced with two stones, a stone in each hand, sim-
> ply to keep your hands down, and with your fists tightly
> clenched. . . . And you had to have an erect carriage, now. At
> the same time, you had to be relaxed, because if you were too
> stiff, of course, it showed in your dancing. So you had to have
> a contradiction in terms; it was paradoxical, I suppose, that it
> was a sort of controlled rigidity of movement. It was relaxation
> on the one hand, and it was rigidly controlled on the other, and
> that's a contradiction in terms, but that's the way it was
> (O'Donovan ctd. in Small).

The most striking feature of Irish dancing for many people is the posture,
a "contradiction in terms," the held upper and moving lower halves of the
body. This is a defining feature of the form, and rarely fails to raise comment among first-time observers. For experienced dancers this feature is
an embodied fundamental that may be discussed in more subtle terms of
rigidity and relaxation, as by well-known traditional step-dancer Joe
O'Donovan above. To maintain a still upper torso and arms while ag-
gressively moving legs and feet is very difficult, requiring a mastery (rigid
control) which, to be convincing, must appear natural (relaxed).

To a beginning Irish dancer, the posture simply is the way it is—an
aspect of the form to be learned. To outsiders, and to dancers in a reflective mood, the posture is more or less a puzzle. Why do Irish dancers
dance that way? Jackie Small, in a radio series on Irish dance music, posed
the question:

> The restricted pose of the Irish solo dancer, with arms rigidly

down by the side, no movement above the waist and so on, looks very strange to people nowadays, accustomed as they are to seeing the freedom of full bodily movement in the various kinds of popular dancing in vogue today and by ballet. What was the reason for this peculiarly inhibited dancing style?

The question reveals a curiosity about the visible discipline of the dance form and the significance of non-movement in a system of expressive movement. Breandán Breathnach, a respected scholar of Irish music and dance traditions, Jackie's guest on this radio program, replies:

I really don't know. I'm sure if you had anthropologists they'd tell you some particular reason why the Irish dance in a particular way, apparently peculiar to themselves—and this was that they dance from the hips down as it were. . . . I'm sure that people would be able to deduce from that that there were particular features of the Irish character manifested by this kind of thing, but I don't know.

On one hand, Breathnach recognizes the anthropological nature of the question, that is, the relation of cultural form to social identity—the fact that Irish dancing has something to do with Irish people. On the other hand, his certainty that anthropologists would give "some particular reason" having to do with "the Irish character" does not instill confidence in the kind of answer that might be provided. Contemporary anthropology would hopefully eschew notions such as "the Irish character," and for that matter the goal of coming up with "some particular reason." It is more likely that a convincing answer will outline various factors and influences as well as subsume simple explanations (e.g., a particular reason) already offered.

The posture is a puzzle, as Small suggests, for two reasons: 1.) because it is non-movement in dancing where we expect more "freedom of full bodily movement"; and 2.) because, as Breathnach suggests, its connection to Irishness is unclear. For Irish dancers and aficionados the puzzle does not need to be resolved in a discursive way. It is enacted, reenacted, solved, and dissolved in the practice of dancing itself. However, for those of us who take a theoretical interest in the form, the question remains. We want to know, along with Jackie Small, "What was the reason for this peculiarly inhibited dancing style?"

In the search for an answer to this question, we might ask ourselves some further questions: Do we want or expect an explanation in terms of cause and effect? (Is there a psycho-cultural cause involving social motivation?) Are we looking for an historical explanation? (What are the origins of this posture? How has it developed?) Is the question one of meaning? (How should one interpret the posture in Irish dancing?) We may actually want answers to all these questions. Why not? Human action is available for each of these analytical "takes." Psychological, historical, social, and cultural dimensions may be inextricably linked in how movement means. Consequently, the reason for this peculiarly inhibited dancing style may turn out to have several analytic dimensions and a plural nature.

Myths

There are stories and explanations offered to account for the remarkable posture. One author traces the style to a ruling by a priest in Donegal who said that hands on hips gave the appearance of haughtiness and suggestiveness (Carty i). Several consultants have explained that since the Catholic Church disapproved of dancing in earlier times, people developed the style of keeping the upper body still so that a priest passing by and glancing in the window could not tell if people were dancing. Another explanation is structurally similar, with hedge schools in penal times as the setting, and British soldiers the disapproving authorities fooled by the non-dancing posture.

An Irish colleague has suggested that these myth-like stories are really examples of Irish humor, jokes, in this case played on the anthropologist who might take them as serious explanations. Interestingly, this very explanation of the myth-like stories reiterates their structure. Once again an outside authority (intellectual, this time) is fooled by Irish folk who may appear to be serious (upper half, not dancing) but are really entertaining themselves (lower half, dancing), this time at the anthropologist's expense. Jokes, of course, work very much like myths. They expose and play with cultural contradictions. In the case of these myths/jokes, the first level of contradiction is the subject of myth—the non-dancing posture in dancing. The second level of contradiction is the subject of joke—the myth-like stories attempt to account for the origins of the posture but are absurd. The joke in essence says: We don't really believe our myths. And this may very well be the case, perhaps a human universal—we don't believe our myths (Veyne), at least not in all circumstances (such as talking to someone from outside our social and cultural structure), even though these same myths/jokes make the world sensible in many other circumstances.

The myth-like quality of these explanations (i.e., explaining origins through narrative) draws attention to some key issues. First, the stories exist as explanations. Thus the posture is recognized as an issue, a puzzle needing solution. Second, the stories recognize the "non-dancing-ness" of the posture that calls attention to itself only in the context of dancing. Its meaning through the window or over the hedge row is precisely not-dancing. Third, these stories attempt to account for the posture in terms of social relations of authority, subordination and, in some cases, resistance. Like myths, these stories and explanations, if unsatisfactory in themselves, contain themes that resonate with historical and contemporary concerns with authority, control, and the morality of expressive body movement.

On a more practical level, some people argue that because the focus of Irish step-dancing is on the feet, the upper body is kept still to minimize distraction. This common-sense explanation has a certain appeal because it sidesteps the problems of social, historical, and semantic investigation. However, this explanation raises questions: why aren't step-dances from other countries, all of which feature the feet, performed with the same posture; and if the purpose of the posture is to avoid distraction from the feet then doesn't it fail in that the posture calls attention to itself as a remarkable feature of the form? The question of meaning cannot be avoided by an appeal to practical reason. There is no natural evolution of dance forms. Irish dancing is a cultural and thus an Irish (including American-Irish, Australian-Irish, and Anglo-Irish) product.

A more recent historical explanation, attributed to a writer for the *Irish Times,* is that girls dancing at the crossroads had to hold their skirts down because it was windy (Wulff). Again, it seems reasonable from one perspective but absurd from others. Why did the arms stay there when it wasn't windy? Why did the boys also dance that way? The explanation is ultimately too nicely simple—the stuff of myth.

Yet there is a grain of truth in both mythical and commonsense explanations. It would be hard to explain their existence if there weren't. Thus any better explanation will have to cast light on these as well. To move toward a more complete explanation more features of context must be included. According to the anthropological principle of holism, a cultural practice cannot be understood except in its relation to other features of the practice and the culture as a whole. One very important aspect of contemporary Irish dancing is its mainly competitive practice.

Competitions

> I cannot bear this regimented [look]. I'm always preaching about being natural and standing to dance as you walk, no strain and no stiffness, you know. And I don't know where this awful sticking out of the chest and keeping [arms] back—I don't know where that all came from. I just don't know. But I'm sorry to say that is the trend as well. That is winning as well. I would go, now, for a good steady dancer with a nice carriage (dance teacher, Galway).

The process of competition adds its own dynamic to the development of Irish dancing. When an aesthetic form such as dancing is placed in the framework of competition, a narrowing of style takes place. It is not a mysterious process. Winners are imitated. Imitation of winning form is one force that narrows the range of style in Irish dancing. The other force is consistent selection of a particular form by adjudicators (dance contest judges). These defining characteristics, as selected by adjudicators, tend to harden and admit less and less variation. For example, at some point crossing the feet became a winning characteristic, so a dancer will not win if he or she does not cross the feet.[1] Thus dancers imitate the winning style, it becomes a defining feature of the form, and is then taught in basic classes. Competitive dancers play a role in this development in imitating winning form and their motivation comes from the competition itself: the motivation to win, above and beyond the motivation to present a dance.

It is the same for the posture, holding the upper body still with back straight, shoulders back, and arms down at the sides: the more straight and still, the better the chances of winning or, perhaps, of not being eliminated. These motivations have an exaggerating effect over time. In order not to be eliminated for points on carriage, dancers tend to make their posture stiff. Teachers develop little techniques to help dancers appear still. For example, young dancers may be taught to keep their hands back behind their hips instead of at their sides. This helps to hide any inadvertent hand movement and also has the effect of exaggerating the protrusion of the chest. As the teacher above put it, "I'm sorry to say that is the trend as well. That is winning as well" (ibid.). And what wins will be imitated, and so it goes, a narrowing and exaggerating of style motivated by competition.

If it is true that a narrowing of style has taken place through the process of competition, then questions arise: what did dancing look like in the past? Were there regional variations? In an article on the position of the hands, a former dancer/teacher and commission member writes about a tradition in Cork of resting the hands on the hips: "in a last effort to win that coveted medal our tradition was discarded and we conformed to the regulations and specifications of modern day competitions" (Cullinane, *Aspects of History* n.p.). While this does not tell us much about the style and posture of Cork step-dancing, it does indicate at least one variation which has been eliminated by the motivations of "modern day competitions."

There is also evidence for a rich and varied past of step-dancing in Ireland in sean-nós, or old-style, step-dancing. Interestingly, participation in this form was until very recently the inverse of modern step-dancing in terms of age and gender, that is, mainly older men performed it. This form has never been institutionalized in regulated or authorized competitions (though there are still a few informal sean-nós step-dancing competitions). The posture style seen in this form varies with the performer, from the same straight back and held arms of modern Irish dancing to a curved spine and moving arms. We can tell from this that it is very unlikely that straight back and still arms was the only style extant in the historical tradition of step-dancing in Ireland.

Imitation of winners is one side of the competitive dynamic that results in narrowing of style choices. The other side, with a different set of motivations, is that a selection has taken place by adjudicators. They select the posture in the process of selecting winners who are then imitated by all competitors.[2] The selection involved is for the notion of "good bearing", a pan-European value.

It is reasonable to assume that adjudicators, especially in the early days of formal competitions, may have felt their selections influenced the way Ireland itself was seen through this symbol—dancing. The fact that the formal organization of Irish dancing grew out of the Gaelic League would indicate that organizers, teachers, and adjudicators were aware of the political dimensions of these activities.[3] The selection of a straight and still posture, seen as "good bearing," in Irish dancing accords with values that accommodate its status as a symbol of the Irish nation, especially in the context of its struggle for political independence. Therefore judges may have selected form, in this case posture, according to broader notions of what is "good". We can ask, why is this "good"? This leads us back to the fact that Irish dancing is a physical education that has its roots in European courtly manners and physical practice.

Manners

The conception of "good posture" manifest in Irish dancing is linked historically with Western European values of comportment and bodily control through what Norbert Elias has called the "civilizing process." Tom Inglis describes this process in the Irish context:

> The modern civilizing process was a transformation of lifestyle, customs and manners. It was a transformation of the body in terms of the mechanisms by which it was controlled.
> . . . It was above all a transformation from open, passionate bodies to closed, moral bodies (140).

In other places in Europe, this process was begun in the imitation of aristocratic behavior by the bourgeoisie. However, in Ireland "it was the Church which was the civilizing force behind the embourgeoisement of the Irish farmer, and because it gained a monopoly of control over their bodies, secular civility became almost synonymous with Catholic morality" (ibid. 165).

The link between the power of the Church and individual bodies or "internally controlled bodies" (Inglis 140) is established through persons who are convinced of the need to effect"self-control" and to encourage or require the same of others, i.e. through personal motivation. But such motivation makes sense only in a social context and cultural rhetoric of moral development. Here is where the Church played a key role. Inglis outlines the various means the Church used to bring about this change in personal motivations. The most important mechanism for inculcating this control was the national school system, established in 1831. Although the national school system was officially secular and the teaching of Catholic doctrine was not permitted, the schools were operated and controlled by the Church:

It was the priests, nuns and brothers, and the teachers under their supervision, who instilled into the uncouth, boorish Irish children of the nineteenth century all the manners and habits which we today regard as standard social practice. . . . They were the forces which girded the bent and unruly bodies of the Irish and fashioned them into fine, *upstanding, moral* citizens (ibid. 157, emphasis added).

There is a primacy given to the body in notions of gentility and also a geometry involved in Western notions of bodily control. These notions have been spelled out in books on manners, some of which, e.g. *Christian Politeness* (1857), were used specifically by the Christian Brothers in their civilizing role in nineteenth-century Ireland:

[I]t is only when the body is controlled that issues such as what is said, and how it is said, come into play. In other words, in social interaction what we do with our bodies takes precedence over what we say. Practice comes before discourse in establishing a person's civility. This is the fundamental characteristic of good manners. For example, as *Christian Politeness* points out, "the head should be kept erect, it should not be turned giddily from side to side". . . The soul is seen as constituted in and through the body as regulated by the head. A regulated head indicates a regulated body (Inglis 161-162).

Spatially, control is a matter of high to low, top to bottom. This schema of control is naturalized in conceptions of body movement. As spatial and bodily metaphors reflect, the verticality of the body and the control with which it is held represent not only the individual's mastery of his or her own body, but a set of social, cultural, and historical values associated with civility, morality, and status. The fact that many of the myth-like explanations of the posture in Irish dancing cite the authority of the Church demonstrates an historical connection and contemporary concern with the morality of expressive body movement—the upper half in the myths. Precisely in the expressiveness of body movement lies the potential for both control and subversion, tradition and change.

Dancing Masters

Itinerant dancing masters of the eighteenth and nineteenth centuries also promoted continental notions of manners and comportment associated with class distinction. Irish dancing teachers today occasionally claim to be carrying on a traditional occupation that extends at least two centuries into the history of Irish society (e.g., Carty 26; Cullinane, *Aspects of History* 26; Judy 14ff). While much of the context of the dancing has changed in various historical periods, the employment of dancing in the service of teaching comportment or social bearing continues.

Nearly all the extant literature on Irish dancing contains references to dancing masters of the eighteenth and nineteenth centuries (Breathnach, *Folk Music;* Cullinane, *Aspects of History*; Carty; O'Rafferty and O'Rafferty; O'Keefe and O'Brien). Often these works refer to "the" dancing master, that is, they describe in general terms the character of this personage rather than actual people and what they did.[4] According to Breathnach, the dancing master was

> a somewhat whimsical figure, pretentious in dress and affecting a grandiloquence not sustained by his schooling. Caroline hat, swallow-tail coat and tight knee-breeches, white stockings and turn-pumps, cane with a silver head and silk tassel—thus accoutered the dancing master was obviously a cut above the wandering piper or fiddler. He was a person to be treated with due deference by his pupils. Good carriage and deportment were his by profession. He considered himself a gentleman, conducted himself as one, and endeavored to instil this spirit into his best pupils (*Folk Music* 49).

Nearly every discussion of "the dancing master" in Irish dancing literature makes reference to his dress, and thus to a certain pretentiousness at least in the rural Irish context.[5] The dancing master is inevitably described as someone who taught more than dancing; he taught a mode of physical conduct with specific references to propriety, civility, a genteel conduct not originating in the indigenous population but imported from courtly custom: "Dancing! Why, it was the least part of what he taught or professed to teach. . . . He taught the whole art o' courtship wid all politeness and success, accordin' as it was practised in Paris durin' the last saison" (Carleton 22-23).

William Carleton's humorous sketch of the Irish country dancing master Buckram-Back is one of the oldest descriptions of such a personage.

Though the extent of its fictionalization is impossible to know, it has served as a model for much of the discussion of dancing masters in the Irish dancing literature, down to the Caroline hat and cane with silk tassel. Carleton's treatment of the dancing master is both a help and hindrance to understanding the importance of his role as tradesman in an advancing hegemony of conduct.[6]

Bodily discipline was (and is) integral to notions of gentility. Courtesy books of the period described how to enter a room, present and receive objects, stand, sit, walk and bow, or curtsey. Dancing was considered the height of bodily mastery. In a chapter entitled "Some observations on the real use and advantages of dancing," the author of *The Polite Academy*, published in 1765, quotes John Locke: "Nothing, says Mr. Locke, in his Treatise of Education, appears to me to give children so much becoming confidence and behaviour, and so to raise them to the conversation of those above their age, as Dancing" (n.p.).

By the nineteenth century this must have been a widely accepted point of view judging by the existence of itinerant dancing masters in not only Ireland but also the British Isles generally, continental Europe, and parts of America. Often they were referred to as "French dancing masters," since Versailles or Paris was regarded as the veritable source of gentility. That their stock in trade was something more than dancing is evident in the words of Locke, in the treatises in courtesy books, as well as in the description by William Carleton. The dancing master offered something people came to believe they needed, whether in rural or urban settings.

Because the dancing master of the past represented an artifice of human being—that is, he taught a mode or style of acting which calls attention to itself as "cultured"—his character was open to a certain ridicule in the "natural" setting of the romantic countryside. Whether a character in a Wycherly play or a Carleton sketch, the dancing master could be depicted as an imperfect representative of the author's own gentility and thus humorously taken to task by noble peasants for attempting to overstep his own place in society through his pretensions. Yet there is something pretentious in all matters of normative manners. Thus the dancing master is portrayed, on the one hand, as "pretentious in dress and affecting a grandiloquence not sustained by his schooling" and, on the other, as "obviously a cut above the wandering piper or fiddler. He was a person to be treated with deference by his pupils." (Breathnach, *Folk Music* 49)

The contradiction is not to be found in real persons—that is, actual dancing masters, about whom we can find out very little prior to 1900 (cf. Cullinane *Aspects of History* 29-35)—so much as in the role, "the" dancing master, as depicted by the genteel Romantic.[7] It is a literary device, one that points out a contradiction in society: manners signify civility, but manners do not make one civil in the deeper sense of thoughtfulness with respect to others. Embedded in this device and its use is a political point of contention between republicanism and aristocracy. Is worth a matter of birth and nature or a matter of learning? Dancing masters (as teachers) representing a republican view though their stock-in-trade is an aristocratic symbol. The Romantic movement of the nineteenth century brought out the inherent contradiction between the pretense of manners and more recently formulated republican ideals.[8]

The dancing master is an important personage, then, both historically and mythologically. Along with the priest, he taught the Irish peasants a new regimen of bodily conduct. This regimen in many ways signified, and in some ways effected, a foreign control and domination of native society and culture, now by the English, now by the Church, and it privileged aristocratic ideals of bodily conduct. At the same time, this version of manners—and the power that it represented—was something the indigenous population came to desire, at least to some extent, and to appropriate.

The (In)Subordination of Dancing

The myths reveal the story of appropriation, resistance, and contradiction embedded in the dance form itself. The Brits and Priests enforce their authority and discipline the unruly Irish bodies, but the dancing goes on. As republican ideals were cemented in the nationalist cultural movement (the Gaelic League), the aristocratic posture was appropriated by Irish dancers as an expression of Irishness. The posture was not only appropriated but has also been hyperbolized in the processes of competition. But many of the accounts of the origin of the posture point back to an earlier imposition of the posture by outside authorities. They point back to the issue of what makes this "good" posture—which in essence is because "they" say so. But what makes good dancing is to move with authority and expression within the confines of the imposed good posture.

The lower body is the site of expression in the sense of dynamic movement, change, and exuberance. In a context where the stillness of the upper body is defined in terms of morality and civility, movement of the lower limbs might seem to represent wildness and subversion. And perhaps it did to some authorities. Indeed, the Church has, off and on throughout the twentieth century, inveighed against the immorality of dancing.[9]

While the opposition of the controlled, moral, held upper body to the wild, subversive, moving lower body may not warrant literal association, it is nonetheless suggested by the dualism inherent in the aesthetic of the divided body: discipline above, dynamics below. In other words, dancers, teachers, and choreographers themselves may not conceive of their movement creations as in any way subversive or opposed to moral strictures. Nor are they. But the relevance of control, authority, and stability above with dynamics, expression, and comment below is nonetheless preserved in their teaching and creations.

As we have already seen, the myth-like stories that account for the origin of the posture provide this "anti-authoritarian" interpretation of danced movement. Contemporary creativity in the movement system continues to challenge the identity of the form, one might say its authenticity, even as it reproduces the posture which remains one of the main identifying features of Irish dancing. Authority and control of the dance form itself are at issue in contests and in theatrical shows as well as in the social organization of Irish dancing.

What, then, of the meaning of movement and the relation between the form of Irish dancing and Irishness itself? Rather than seeing particular features of "the Irish character," we have found recurring themes in myth, in history, and in aspects of contemporary practice.

I will attempt an answer to Jackie Small's question posed at the beginning of the chapter, i.e., "what was the reason for this peculiarly inhibited dancing style?" What is Irish about this posture is the contemporary salience of these themes incorporated (literally, in + corpore) in contrasting halves of the Irish dancing body: imposition and rebellion, control and exuberance, stasis and change, order and dynamism. These, of course, are very general terms and can be further interpreted according to political, moral, social, historical, institutional, and other concerns, as indeed we shall see in subsequent chapters. But to specify any one set of meanings would be to collapse the semantic multi-dimensionality of body movement gratuitously.

CHAPTER TWO

Dancing as National Expression

*I have said again and again that when the Gaelic League was
founded in 1893 the Irish Revolution began.*
—Padraig Pearse, 1914

Step-dancing in Ireland became "Irish dancing" in 1893, the same year
that Pearse cites as the beginning of the Irish Revolution. The signal event
was the founding of the Gaelic League, perhaps the most important mile-
stone in modern Irish history and, not coincidentally, the history of Irish
dancing. Between approximately 1880 and 1910 a paradigmatic shift occurred in Irish culture. Expressive forms, from sports to spoken language,
became politicized. During this period "Irish dancing" emerged as a category, a genre of dancing. Solo step-dancing was already a widely known
practice. Dancing masters had been teaching the form in Ireland since at
least the eighteenth century (Hutton 446-447). At this time, however, the
dancing took on new meaning. Solo step-dancing and an invented social
dance form called *céilí* were combined under the nationalist designation,
"Irish dancing", and took on new significance in opposition to other forms
designated as foreign.

Thus Irish dancing, at least in name, had its origin in the foundational
work of the Gaelic League. In addition, this new nationalist designation
of the form provided a necessary ingredient to the institutional organization of Irish dancing and the modern competitive model through which
the form developed and is practiced today. [1]

Nationalism and the Politics of Culture
Political historians seem to agree (e.g., Lyons, Ireland 27-55; Garvin, Evolution 89-91) that after the fall of Parnell and the Home Rule movement
in 1890 the resulting political vacuum was soon filled by a nationalist cultural movement. The period, often referred to as the Gaelic Revival, can

be bracketed by the founding of the Gaelic Athletic Association (G.A.A.) in 1884 and, for our purposes, the founding of An Coimisiún le Rincí Gaelacha, The Irish Dancing Commission, in 1929.[2]

The G.A.A., initiated by the Irish Republican Brotherhood (Mandle, "I.R.B." and *Sport;* Puirséal 33-40), carried from its inception a political message reflected in the following article published in 1885 in United Ireland by one of the founders, Michael Cusack:

> No movement having for its object the social and political advancement of a nation from the tyranny of imported and enforced customs and manners can be regarded as perfect if it has not made adequate provision for the preservation and cultivation of the national pastimes of the people (qtd. in Puirséal 37).

The Gaelic Athletic Association organized young men into hurling and football clubs. While the purpose was athletic entertainment, it was also a secular organization based on parish lines that provided a fertile recruiting ground for nationalist causes, including military organizations (Garvin, *Evolution* 65-66).

Conradh na Gaeilge, (The Gaelic League), founded a decade later, initially proclaimed itself non-political. However, its message of cultural revival could never be separated from the context of political and cultural domination in which such a movement was deemed necessary. At its annual convention in 1915, militants managed to pass a resolution committing the League to the support of "a free Ireland." With this move the League was brought "firmly under the control of the advanced nationalists" (Comerford 32; Nowlan 44, 50). This takeover resulted in the resignation of its president and founder, Douglas Hyde, who had desired to keep the movement overtly apolitical, even if for politically practical reasons (Garvin, "Nationalist" 80). The revival of Irish spoken and written language, music, dancing, and games in the context of foreign domination could not help but take on political significance whether overtly intended or not.

The Gaelic League was organized around the idea of language promotion. The steady decline in the number of native Gaelic speakers since the famine was seen as a threat to nationhood itself. Douglas Hyde expressed this view—in a way that caught the imagination of many a listener and reader—suggesting a connection between individual responsibility and national identity. He made the case innumerable times, not least in his famous lecture to the National Literary Society in 1892, "The Necessity for De-Anglicizing Ireland":

> It has always been curious to me how Irish sentiment sticks in this half-way house—how it continues to apparently hate the English and at the same time continues to imitate them; how it continues to clamour for recognition as a distinct nationality, and at the same time throws away with both hands what would make it so (qtd. in Lyons, *Ireland* 228).

Hyde's remedy was to revive the language, customs, and games from Ireland's native past. Irish forms of music and dancing were promoted along with the language as part of the unique cultural heritage that defined the nation. Traveling Gaelic League teachers taught dances, history, folklore, and music in addition to language. They also organized *feiseanna, céilithe,* and *aeríochtaí* (festivals, dances, and open-air entertainments) (MacAodha 22). The League thus provided the means for individuals to act in response to Hyde's rhetoric of responsibility. Participation in dancing and language classes was a way to directly involve oneself in the de-anglicization and preservation of Ireland.

In the case of each of these expressive cultural activities, the form promoted by the Gaelic League (and/or the G.A.A.) was defined in opposition to a "foreign" form, usually meaning English.

> Anything English was ipso facto not for the Irish, as it might appear to weaken the claim to separate nationhood, but any valued cultural possessions of the English were shown to have their Gaelic equivalents. Thus was born what Seán de Fréine has acutely called an ingenious device of national parallelism:[4]
>
>
>
> English language — Irish language
>
> English law — Brehon law
>
> Parliament — Dáil
>
> Prime Minister — Taoiseach
>
> Soccer — Gaelic football
>
> Hockey — Hurling
>
> Trousers — Kilt
>
>
>
> It mattered little whether those devices had a secure basis in Irish history, for if they had not previously existed they could be invented (Kiberd 151).[5]

So intense was the G.A.A. rejection of foreign sports that members were not allowed to play rugby or soccer: "the rejection of foreign games may be seen as an expression of that remarkable crusading spirit, to be found in the Gaelic League as well, that sought by active means to save the nation from Anglicization" (Nowlan 43).

In the early years of the Irish Dancing Commission a similar rule was in effect. Member dancers and teachers were not allowed to attend dances other than Irish dances (MacConuladh, *An Coimisiún* 2). Participation in these activities became a declaration of political alignment and, as far as the official organizations were concerned, there could be no room for ambiguity. Either one was aligned with the nationalist movement through participation in the cultural forms that were held to be "natural" symbols of the Irish nation, or one was aligned with foreign interests.

Irish Dancing: A New Genre with Claims to Antiquity

A look at the fifty to one hundred years that preceded the Gaelic revival reveals very little about the genres of dancing extant in Ireland. There appears to be a dearth of writing on dancing during this time. Often the people who mentioned dancing in historical texts, if they categorized dance forms at all, did not describe the dancing they saw (e.g., Young). Most writers on Irish customs were travelers who brought a foreign perspective that paid scant attention to native categories (Moryson and Dineley cited in Breathnach, *Folk Music* 38-39; Cullinane, *Aspects of History* 7-9). We do know that there were traveling dancing masters, although most accounts describe only social settings and distinguishing personal characteristics. Virtually none describe the dancing they taught, for the very good reason that movement description defies spoken and written language capabilities.[6]

Many problems arise in the effort to trace genres or styles of dance backward in time. Without some means of recording movement, not to mention understanding its formal structure, it is impossible to know what sorts of matchings exist between linguistic terms employed for categories of movements and various movement practices themselves.[7] Scholars who have written on the history of dancing in Ireland have all confronted this problem (e.g., Breathnach, *Folk Music* 38-43; Cullinane, *Aspects of History* 6-10).

Many historians do not address the form of dancing so much as accepted genres of music (jig, reel, and hornpipe). However, any belief that musical and dance forms are inextricably linked in their origins is belied by consideration of the "sets" which appear to be of foreign origin yet are danced to local jigs, reels, and hornpipes, as well as to Irish polkas and slides, some of which are themselves distinctly Irish adaptations of foreign musical forms. In addition to problems regarding the linkage of musical forms to dance forms is the even more trenchant problem of the linkage of verbal forms to both. Contemporary use of the word "set" illustrates the problem.

In the contemporary world of dancing within Ireland, the word "set" can mean: 1.) a genre of social dancing; 2.) a sub-genre of step-dancing; 3.) a genre of music for step-dancing; 4.) a group of dancers; 5.) a group of movements done by a group of dancers; or 6.) a phrase of movements performed by a solo dancer. Each meaning is dependent upon its specific context. Notice that the word describes two varieties of dancing and one

Potential Confusion Regarding the Word "Set" in the Context of Dancing in Ireland

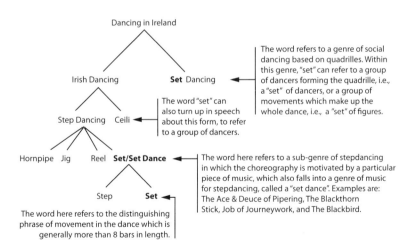

2. **The word "set" in the context of Irish dancing.** This chart shows why linguistic tags cannot be relied upon for a consistent meaning with respect to movement.

of music and, further, that one of the dance forms is linked in practice to the music form of that name while the other one is not [Fig. 2.].

Whatever escapes our direct knowledge of the earlier nineteenth century, it is clear that the Gaelic revival of the late nineteenth century spawned a great deal of interest in dancing, especially identifying *Irish* dancing, making distinctions with respect to so-called foreign forms of dancing, and recording "Irish dances." In 1902 two texts appear: *A Handbook of Irish Dances* by J. G. O'Keeffe and A. O'Brien; and *A Guide to Irish Dancing*, by J. J. Sheehan. Both are instruction manuals with descriptions of steps and figures for the social dances which have since come under the rubric of "ceili dances." These include four-, eight-, twelve- and sixteen-hand reels and jigs, as well as some "country dances." The books also include short essays on the origins and histories of jigs, reels, and hornpipes.

> To the jig must be awarded the honour of being our oldest national dance; and there cannot be any doubt that of all the dances known in Ireland at the present day the jig has the best title to the description "traditional."
>
> O'Curry suggested the word "jig" was derived from the Italian "gigue," and thereupon many people who ought to have known better assumed that the jig had an Italian origin. It is easy to see how the mistake arose.
>
> Hardiman tells us (quoting Tassoni) that the ancient music of Ireland was *imitated* by Gesualdus, the "chief of the Italian composers and greatest musical improver of the sixteenth century"—a fact which ought to be sufficient to dispose of the "Italian origin" theory regarding the jig. As if that were not enough, one English authority states that the first known dance tune in English, dating back to 1300, was a kind of jig, and it is certain the English didn't invent it (Sheehan 4, emphasis in original).

Putting aside the logic of the argument and validity of its claims, we see a central concern with the authenticity of uniquely Irish cultural forms.[8] The author makes an argument for original invention set in the context of cultural borrowings by other (already accepted) nationalities, the English and Italians. These concerns set the tone for much of the scholarship on dancing in Ireland for the twentieth century. Origins, ownership, borrowings, and exchanges of dance and musical forms between nationalities are the topics that repeatedly turn up in discussion (see Breathnach, *Folk Music;* Cullinane, *Aspects of History* and *Further Aspects; and* Carty). While the origins of various kinds of dancing in Ireland may elude researchers, the origin of the printed *discussion of origins* appears to be in 1902 with the publication of booklets by O'Keefe and O'Brien, and Sheehan.

The heritage of step-dancing was evidently unquestioned by members of the Gaelic League, although indigenous origins would be very difficult to prove. For example, a factor that may indicate a foreign origin for step-dancing would be the existence of dancing masters, a continental European phenomenon during the preceding century in Ireland. However, since the introduction of step-dancing preceded the limits of contemporary living memory, its pedigree was not at issue. Another dance form, a social form called "set dancing" (from "sets of quadrilles") diffused through Ireland within the preceding century. Their introduction in living memory may have raised the issue of origins. While the Gaelic League evidently recognized the power of social dancing to attract people to their movement (Carolan 8; Comerford 35; MacAodha 23), there remained the question of the *Irishness* of various social dance forms.

Social dances adopted as Irish by the Gaelic League were given the name c*éilí* while "the sets" were held to be of foreign origin, thus not truly Irish.[9] Sets were believed by some to have been introduced by soldiers following the Napoleonic War. Thus the separate genre of ceili dances was created by its placement in opposition to the sets.

It is nearly impossible to trace two distinct forms—ceili and sets—regressively into the eighteenth century. Two contemporary scholars (Carolan; and Cullinane, *Aspects of History*) take up this very issue and make separately convincing arguments regarding possible developments. Carolan traces the development of ceili dances through the London Gaelic League.[10] What is perhaps more interesting than their narrative of the origin, is the confirmation of their pre-existing belief that such Irish social dances had existed:

> For the particularly interested League members the new
> dances introduced by Reidy came as proof of something they
> *had always believed:* that group social dances other than

dances of the quadrille type had once been part of the Irish tradition (Carolan 9, emphasis added).

Here we see the logic of national parallelism at work. Wherever the dances actually come from is secondary to the place they occupy in the symbology and beliefs of nationalists.

Cullinane offers a different account based on oral histories. He speculates that the histories of sets and ceili dances merge. He accounts for the differences between the forms by arguing that ceili dances bear the stamp of influence of dancing masters (higher order of discipline) more than the localized traditions of sets:

> I believe that the Quadrilles and other dances (Lancers etc.) were introduced into Ireland and came to be danced to faster music and to Irish tunes when they came under the Irish influence. The dancing masters introduced a greater degree of discipline and solo dancing into "some" [sic] of these dances. The less altered of these are what we now refer to as the sets and the more evolved-disciplined ones which became more formalised under the influence of the dancing masters and later on the Gaelic League then became known as "Ceilí." There is no clear cut line of distinction between the sets and the Ceilí dances, the Ceilí dances are simply a more evolved disciplined form. The distinction between the two forms has only become more pronounced since 1900 approximately onwards (when the term Ceilí dances was invented) (Cullinane, *Aspects of History* 24).

The discipline and formalizing influence that Cullinane attributes to the dancing master results in a sophistication and intricacy that requires teaching and training. Against this, set dancing appears considerably easier: "The lack of intricacies in the movements and the general liveliness and frivolity usually associated with the performance of these sets have made them extremely popular, for such is their construction that almost anyone can join in" (ibid. 14).[11]

These points map a very different field of debate than that of Sheehan, O'Keefe, and O'Brien in 1902. Carolan and Cullinane begin with the recognition of the significance of the Gaelic League in the history of Irish dancing. Cullinane's point, that dancing masters may have introduced more physical discipline into the form which came to be known as "ceili" would account for a formal similarity with step-dancing, the Irish origins of which had always been assumed.

Whatever the explanation for their origins or history, during the decades around the turn of the century ceili dances emerged as a distinct and approved form parallel to the sets in social function but with national identification. The Gaelic League promoted and taught them with huge success. Indeed it has been suggested that more people learned to dance under the educational efforts of the Gaelic League than ever learned to speak the Irish language (MacAodha 23).

While the ceili dancing became very popular on its own as a social activity of the Gaelic League, both the ceili and step-dancing were also promoted via competitions. Bringing these forms into the competitive model of social event worked further changes on the dancing. In addition, a change in the model of competition itself resulted from the introduction of forms claimed to have national significance.

Irish Dancing Becomes an Institution

As far as national identity of the expressive forms is concerned, the most important change during the period of the Gaelic Revival was the identification of the genre of Irish dancing itself. But the second most important change had to be, in my opinion, the formal organization of Irish dancing competitions under the central control of an Irish Dancing Commission.

It is nearly impossible to separate Irish solo step-dancing and competition. As far back as memories, records, and legends go there have been competitions of one sort or another between dancing masters, their pupils, or simply people with clever feet. Contests were said to be part of county fairs or markets, and they were a part of pub culture, house dances, and informal home entertainment generally. Modern Irish step-dancing, however, has undergone formal organizational development. The shift from local competitions to a nationally-organized competitive model depended upon a nationalist vision and centralized organization. Furthermore, once established, this organization reinforced a nationalist vision of the dance as an institution in both its social organization and body movement form.

The Gaelic League chose to promote interest in Irish cultural forms by sponsoring competitions. According to its publication, *An Claidheamh*

Soluis (Sword of Light), the first feis under its auspices was conducted in Macroom on 09 April 1899. An advertisement for the feis announced: "The competitions include a written essay on the life of Thomas Davis, recitations, ballads and folk songs, narration of folklore, reel, jig and horn-pipe dancing" (ctd. in Cullinane, *Further Aspects* 37).

The term *feis* was used by the Gaelic League to invoke the Gaelic/Celtic past when feiseanna (pl.) were parliamentary assemblies that were accompanied by sporting events, games, and entertainments of various sorts. Under the Gaelic League (and later An Coimisiún le Rincí Gaelacha), *feis* came to mean competition as well as festival, for competitive events may have been the focal point of the gatherings. Still, a celebratory atmosphere with music sessions in pubs might also surround official activities at a feis.

The early feiseanna held under the auspices of the Gaelic League were locally organized and administered. For example, one held in Miltown Malbay, Co. Clare in 1899 had a rule that only Irish speakers could compete in the step-dancing. At the time this was a predominately Irish-speaking area (Cullinane, *Further Aspects* 38). Rules were made for the competitions by local organizers. Adjudicators were selected according to the organizers' varying conceptions of what was required for a contest. It was not always the case that adjudicators were accomplished dancers themselves. Indeed, Cullinane reports that at the first Oireachtas (national competition) organized by the Gaelic League in 1897, the official adjudicators were well-known members of the League and that "it is extremely unlikely that they were either dancers or knew much about dancing" (ibid. 41).

It might seem strange that non-dancers could have been selected to evaluate a dancing competition. At the time, however, it would seem that the promotion of Irishness took precedence over the finer points of distinction between dance performances. As the Gaelic League had taken the lead in calling attention to Irish manners, customs, and Irishness itself, they were the authorities, even if self-proclaimed, on tradition. By this logic they were capable of adjudicating an *Irish* dancing competition even though they may not have been dancers themselves.

This circumstance allowed for much debate on the qualifications of judges, the fairness of competitions, and the categories of evaluation. The competitive model which had been in place during this early phase of the

Gaelic revival worked well enough at the local level where rules had only to make sense to those participating, and questions of standards need only be reconciled with local culture, society, and politics. Negotiation of standards at the local level evidently included fisticuffs and grudges on occasion (MacConuladh, "Origin"). Members of the Gaelic revival found this embarrassing. The Gaelic League was also a "civilizing" movement in many ways (Chapter One), bringing a message of self-discipline and control to a population it viewed as "degenerate" in ways: another result of Anglicization. Thus it was only natural for the Gaelic League to see such local altercations as counter-productive to the larger vision of the League. During this time the spread of nationalist ideology, along with the revival of interest in expressive forms, provided the persuasive vantage point from which the older localized competitive model could be challenged and a new, unified, and national model justified.

The concept of nation creates a point of view above the local, from which local customs can be criticized and found wanting.[12] The logic goes like this: if the nation is one distinct community conceived according to the model of one individual, one body, then isn't there also one Irish dancing, one unified movement symbol? By implication, shouldn't there be one set of rules by which Irish dancing is to be adjudicated? The authority of local approaches can be called into question by this appeal to a higher-level arbiter of identity. This is precisely the conclusion a disappointed competitor might reach when losing at a feis in the next parish or county. The local organizers and adjudicators can be accused of favoring their own neighbors and not rewarding the best dancer, even more, the best *Irish* dancer:

> Irregularities of all sorts were common and fierce disputes frequently occurred at dancing competitions, even violence and threats of violence being not unknown. Since all or nearly all competitions at that time were at Feiseanna and other events organised by An Conradh [The Gaelic League] that organization soon became perturbed as the irregularities and rows connected with dancing tended to bring its Feiseanna into disrepute (MacConuladh, "Origin" 1).

The Gaelic League in 1929 appointed a commission (*Coimisiún na Rinnce*, Commission on Dance) to look into and make recommendations with respect to these problems in the dancing competitions. This body, just a few years later, became *An Coimisiún le Rincí Gaelacha* (The Irish Dancing Commission), empowered to enforce its own recommendations:

> (a) do everything necessary to promote Irish dancing, both ceili and stepdancing; (b) exercise *central control* on Irish dancing and those connected with it, teachers, adjudicators, pupils and organisers of competitions; (c) draw up all rules necessary for those purposes and enforce the implementation of those rules (MacConuladh ibid., emphasis added).

With this move the Gaelic League institutionalized the dancing (ceili and step-dancing) under its own auspices. Like the League, An Coimisiún defined itself in terms of promoting cultural form, but it also centralized authority and set before itself the task of codifying the rules of participation and production of this form. Furthermore, An Coimisiún maintained the alliance with the Gaelic League. One-half of the Commission members were appointed by the Gaelic League; the other half were representatives elected by various dancing teachers' organizations, an arrangement that continues in smaller proportion today.[13]

Breakaway Organizations

The ideal of a centralized authority that would look after the practice of Irish dancing made sense according to nationalist logic. But in practice there were conflicts of interest. The early meeting notes of the *Coimisiún na Rinnce* show that there were two extant teachers' organizations, one in Dublin and one in Cork. The Commission dealt with them very differently. At a meeting in July 1932 a motion was put before the Commission that no teacher (presumably in Dublin) would be registered who wasn't also registered in the Dublin Teachers' Organization, a friendly move toward the Dublin T.O. The motion passed at the following meeting, and at that same meeting the Commission decided to ask for a report on the Cork Teachers' Organization from the Cork branch of the Gaelic League. At a September meeting of the same year it was moved that the Commission disassociate from the Cork T.O. and only deal with local Cork teachers through the Gaelic League, an unfriendly move toward the Cork T.O. An attempt was made to bring into alignment these different approaches to the two city-based teachers' organizations by a further motion: to end all dance teachers' associations and have all authority and control vested in the

Commission only ("Minutes" of An Coimisiún, 1932).

The conflicts that were evident in these early meetings followed two divisions in the relations of Irish dancing production. One division was between dance teachers and non-teachers. Organizations of dancing teachers in Cork and Dublin also represent a center-periphery division, as Dublin was the strong political center of the Gaelic League. These two tensions, between teachers and what we might call "cultural brokers" (non-dance-expert Gaelic League members), and between the political center of Dublin and the outlying areas, were built into the structure of the Irish Dancing Commission through its founding by the Gaelic League. Eventually the first tension led to a split when in 1969 a number of teachers instituted a rival organization, *Comhdháil Muinteoirí na Rincí Gaelacha* (Congress of Irish Dance Teachers).[14] This organization set up its own competitions, teacher and adjudicator exams, membership, rules, and so forth. In other words, it reproduced the model of a national organization of competitive Irish dancing, but this one under the control of the dancing teachers alone.

This was not the only split the Commission endured. In 1951 a teacher from Belfast was suspended for participating in an event at which "God Save the Queen" was performed. Patricia Mulholland resolved not to go back to the Commission after her six-month suspension and instead joined the Festival Association of Northern Ireland. She also began The Irish Ballet, blending Irish dancing and ballet to dramatize stories from Irish mythology. Part of her self-definition and professional success is her ability to work "across the divide," Protestant and Catholic ("I've had a mixed company all my life."). Her appearance in settings bearing symbols of England, the nation-defining "other," raised the issue of dichotomous affiliation (with us or against us) in the nationalist rhetoric of the Gaelic League and its offspring, the Irish Dancing Commission. Once the League became overtly political, this kind of either/or vantage point could be argued as threatening to the very identity of the organization and the dancing. It wasn't necessary to so argue, but it always could be so argued within a nationalist sensibility.[15] Whether the disagreement was ideological or not, and there are varying accounts, the point is that the Gaelic League rhetoric (either/or) and structure (not just dancers, but Irishness experts on the Commission) allowed for this kind of split as well.

Although Patricia Mulholland began an "Irish Ballet," she did not leave behind the world of competitive dancing. The Festival Association also took up Irish dancing competitions. Teaching and training in Irish dancing included competitions with affiliated teachers, adjudicators, rules, and so forth. The ballet was mainly for dancers who were finished with competition. The Irish Ballet was a development of Irish dancing; it was not identified *as* Irish dancing per se. The model of competition thus transcended the social and political split from *An Coimisiún*.

As dramatic and different as both of these breakaway events and organizations were, the interesting feature for this analysis is that they both retained the agonistic model in the practice of Irish dancing. The particular history of the emergence of the category "Irish dancing" shows it wedded to nationalist ideology and to competition. Furthermore, the formal social relations that were created with the Irish Dancing Commission made possible a new model of competition—modern institutionalized competition.

The Modern Competitive Model

When *An Coimisiún le Rincí Gaelacha* organized, it immediately effected a change in the social relations of production in Irish dancing. Authority was now located in a central organization that would attempt to control the people involved in Irish dancing, the events, and the form itself. This would be accomplished by methods of certification, sanctioning, and otherwise expressing approval of certain people as teachers, adjudicators, and qualified participants in its events. In addition it would exercise control over its events by codifying and enforcing rules.

In establishing an institutional practice of Irish dancing-as-competition, *An Coimisiún* was following a model that had been developed throughout Britain in the Victorian era, the model of modern sport. This included codification of rules, a hierarchical structure of competitions based on local, county, provincial, and national levels, as well as an ascription to the activity of high moral purpose, as both education in and expression of national ideals (Mandle "Games"; and "Gaelic Athletic").

The Irish Dancing Commission followed the pattern established in Ireland by the G.A.A. that organized Irish sports as institutionalized practice and public entertainment. Games played with referees, umpires, and other officials, enforcing a unified set of rules before increasingly large audiences, replaced local versions of hurling and football which previously had taken as many forms as the localities in which they were played.

The model of modern competition developed in sport reflected idealized versions of social relations and cultural values of modern industrial society:

> Organised sport . . . sprang from the society that nurtured and supported it. I suggest that its framework, organisation, ethics, even its quirks and quiddities, were nineteenth century industrial. In organised sport we see the inventor, the entrepeneur, the employee, the class conflict. Whatever you like to name as part of Victorian industrial society was there: its passion for classification, order and detail, for moralising, for self-improvement, for respectability (Mandle, "Games" 512).

Ireland itself was not a heavily industrialized society at the turn of the century, but the cultural environment in which contemporary political ideas were formed was Victorian. And, of course, the notion of "fair competition" itself is an idealization pulled from the legitimizing rhetoric of a political economy based on competition, itself an international force articulated at national, regional, and local levels. Fair competition, in the context of producing a national symbol in dance, requires a national-level codification of rules and authentication of competitions, adjudicators, and dancers.

The modern model of competition provided a means of promotion and control over the practice of Irish dancing for the Gaelic League; and it provided an ideological structure which instantiated its national level of significance regardless of the social level of practice (local, regional, national, international). However, it was the context of the Gaelic revival, the Irish Ireland movement that spanned the last quarter of the nineteenth and first quarter of the twentieth centuries, that begat Irish dancing. The nationalist cultural movement infused the practice of step-dancing with political and cultural identity lasting into the next century. In many ways, though, the modern mode of competition has had even more profound effects on the form and its practice.

CHAPTER THREE

Dancing as Competition

In the sitting room of a teacher's home during the World Championships of Irish dancing, a group of teachers, adjudicators and family members have tea, trading stories and laughter. One story concerned a teacher who became physically ill at the provincial championship when one of her students didn't get a recall (i.e., high enough marks from the adjudicators in the first round to be asked back for the final round of the competition):

> Didn't I stop what I was doing and go to her?! And the others! We all went down to her. Ah, but there was another present, giving out the whole time, "How unfair 'tis! How corrupt the adjudication! And isn't such and such adjudicator staying in the home of your first place teacher?" And all the time the blood pressure was rising. A doctor came and saw the patient, but the madwoman wouldn't leave the room, all the time giving out, she was. The doctor finally came out and said the patient would live—unless the mad one killed her with her bother. [laughter] Says the doctor, "I have but one question. What is a 'recall'?" [peals of laughter] Says he, "I thought it had something to do with a seance! [laughter] Your one kept muttering about 'the recall.'" The doctor said whatever else happened that night, he learned he would never send his little ones to Irish dancing! [more laughter] (Teacher, Limerick, 1991)

The storytellers laugh at themselves, the seriousness with which they take this business of dancing. "Sure we're all mad, Frank." In this story the woman who becomes physically ill at the disappointment of defeat is well understood by the other teachers. They go to her side and even call a doctor. The "madwoman" brings up an always present and dangerous suspicion that the competition is not fair. The sick woman doesn't need this commentary at this time. The doctor, the objective outsider, recognizes the madness of the haranguer and of Irish dancing itself, both of which are the occasion of the present drama and enjoyment.

The stories themselves are an enjoyment. They organize conflicting values and passions into a moment of lucidity including a critical appreciation of competition, its social and cultural effects, and the proper way to handle them. Stories and humor often point to serious issues or contradictions with which people must live. For example, this story points to the emotional and mental stress that can be felt by an individual teacher when one of her students fails, perhaps in a competition where she was expected to do well. It also points to the subjective element in aesthetic competitions, that human judges decide who wins and that humans are corruptible. In a manner of speaking, the stories say that, yes, these pressures and contradictions are there but it is better to laugh them off than let them get you down. And laughing at them together, over tea and biscuits, brings a feeling of shared contradictions. It brings out the social nature of the individual feelings.

The whole event of an Irish dancing competition, whether the World Championships or a local *feis* (competition), is a very social one as people come together to experience the drama of dance contests. Competitions can be great fun and excitement for the participants, be they teachers, dancers, or relatives of dancers. But at the heart of these social occasions is the game: it is an aesthetic game, an expressive game, but foremost a game. Levi-Strauss points out that while social rituals have a conjoining social effect, bringing people together in a shared status, competitions have an inverse effect:

> Games thus appear to have a disjunctive effect: they end in the establishment of a difference between individual players or teams where originally there was no indication of inequality. And at the end of the game they are distinguished into winners and losers. . . . Asymmetry is engendered: it follows inevitably from the contingent nature of events, themselves due to intention, chance or talent . . . the game produces events by means of a structure (32).

Even while the feis is a social occasion, it also creates social rifts, distinctions, differences in value between otherwise equals. In this way it is like any modern sport, a structure (rules and roles defined in a social institution) that produces events (*feiseanna*, contests, and their results). The sports analogue would be a league, its referees, teams, coaches, and players. In Irish dancing it is An Coimisiún, its adjudicators, schools, teachers, and dancers. When the beginner takes lessons she enters a social structure that is organized around the competitive process: "I mean everybody dances competitively; there's no way out of dancing competitively. Kids from three years of age up until my age, you have to dance competitively. 'Cause that's mainly what Irish dancing is about" (Dancer, age 20, Cork, 1991).

Competition has helped to define the dancing since the turn of the last century when the Gaelic League decided to promote various Irish cultural forms through contests. This is a fact impinging upon all others in the expressive form, the movement system itself, and the social practice of the dancing. Even shows like *Riverdance* would not exist were it not for formal, institutionalized competitions that have driven the development of Irish dancing to such impressive heights.

Is competition good or bad? Both. It is good for some things and bad for others. This is a perspective gleaned from dancers, teachers, and other participants themselves. Competition produces good effects and bad, good motivations and bad; it even produces a dance form itself that is good in some ways and bad in others, but always relative to some particular perspective or question.

It must be said that reflective consideration of competition is far from constant. At competitions themselves, participants in various roles are likely to be so rapt in the process that they would be unlikely to even consider competition in the abstract. In reflective consideration, competition may be positively valued, especially as an educational activity, for preparing children to enter a "real world" of competition while helping them to build confidence. This sort of view of a real world makes sense in a society and culture with a competition-based economy, an economy that produces winners and losers from a material perspective. Competitive games of all sorts permeate Western cultures and constitute an increasingly important modern ritual and spectacle. While the ideology of a competitive market economy does not explain the various sports and games that exist, it does show why these sorts of games resonate as analogy, and thus preparation, for the "real world."

Competition is recognized as a powerful force in itself and is entrenched in Irish dancing. Consequently, its beneficial and challenging aspects have to be managed by dancers, their parents and other relatives, as well as by teachers, adjudicators, and Coimisiún members. This requires ongoing work that permeates learning, teaching, and doing the dance movement as well as judging and administering the competitive events and institutions. As the subject of this chapter, the management of forces and motivations engendered by the practice of competition will be considered with respect to commission members first, then teachers with their dancers and parents, and finally, adjudicators.

Members of An Coimisiún occupy the top position in the *hierarchical organization* of Irish dancing. They make the rules as well as register judges, teachers, and dancers for purposes of competing in Coimisiún-sanctioned events. However teachers occupy the central position in the *social network* of Irish dancing with other schools spread across the country and globe, and between the official institution and the dancers themselves with their parents. The adjudicator occupies the central position in the competition as an *event*. Therefore, in considering these three social positions and the specific pressures at work upon them, we gain an understanding of the enduring, i.e., structural, features of Irish dancing competition. It should be remembered that these are social roles or positions and not persons, per se, that are discussed here. One person can occupy all three statuses and thus feel various and conflicting pressures depending on which of these statuses is most salient in a given context.

Irish Dancing Commission Members

A feature of Irish dancing is the extent to which it is competition orientated as compared with the national dancing of other countries. It is said at times that competitions are far too frequent and extensive and there is probably a degree of truth in the allegation. However, competitions are seemingly much in demand by teachers, pupils and parents alike and it cannot be denied that competitions have played a very significant part in bringing our national dancing to the high stage of development it has attained today (MacConuladh, *An Coimisiún* 1).

This text from an official pamphlet of An Coimisiún reveals an ambivalence towards competition as the prevalent activity and orientation of the dancing. On the one hand, the role of competition in shaping the form of modern Irish dancing, especially the degree of technique and skill required, "cannot be denied." Yet it is "too frequent and extensive." Although this phrase is not explained, the sense is that competition has somehow overtaken in importance other meaningful aspects of Irish dancing, perhaps its importance as a national representation, as the comparison with other national dancing suggests. The fact that an official description of the organization acknowledges this criticism shows the extent to which the organizers themselves recognize a dilemma in the activity. Nevertheless, the demand for competitions comes from the membership; therefore official uneasiness is simply noted and balanced by the recognition of the "high stage of development" brought to Irish dancing by the practice of competition.

As we saw in the previous chapter, An Coimisiún le Rincí Gaelacha came into existence to regulate Irish dancing competitions. Their mission as developed by a Gaelic League Committee on Irish dancing was to:

> (a) do everything necessary to promote Irish dancing, both ceili and stepdancing; (b) exercise central control on Irish dancing and those connected with it, teachers, adjudicators, pupils and organisers of competitions; (c) draw up all rules necessary for those purposes and enforce the implementation of those rules (MacConuladh, "Origin" 1).

In effect, the work of the commission appears to have been taken up with items (b) and (c). Promotion of Irish dancing has been left to the appeal of competitions themselves, and this has been quite successful. The aesthetic game has attracted and kept great numbers of participants in Ireland and the diaspora. However, non-competitive versions of ceili and step-dancing have moved increasingly outside the concern of An Coimisiún. The only major events that the commission has instituted are annual competitions—Oireachtas Rince na hEireann (All-Ireland Championships) and Oireachtas Rince na Cruinne (World Championships) on Easter weekend every year.

While it might seem that An Coimisiún is in a position to influence the course of development in Irish dancing, the motivations of competition seem to overwhelm any initiative that is not specifically reactionary to an issue relating to competitions themselves. I was told repeatedly by members that their highest aspirations for An Coimisiún are continually frustrated by the need to take care of what many of them consider to be the petty business of administering the competitive institution generally (and specifically the All-Ireland and World Championships), dealing with rules, appeals, special cases in the application of rules such as the transfer rule (discussed below under Teachers), arguments and accusations between people in their various roles as teachers and adjudicators, and so on.[1]

Attempts to handle such projects as rewriting the ceili handbooks (*Ar Rinncidhe Foirne*) or making a video of ceili dances are typically constrained by the exigencies of competitions. Indeed, the books are to be rewritten, not to promote these dances or make them accessible to wider audiences, but to serve as *definitive* descriptions for purposes of judging ceili competitions. In essence, this will be a project to turn what was originally a collection of country dances for dissemination as promotion of national culture into a "bible" for competition, a text of the definitive version for each dance, ultimately to resolve disputes with adjudicators' choices. Only competition could have generated the need for such a text. Only competition could require an aesthetic form to be so officially defined.

An Coimisiún itself is comprised mostly of teachers, elected to their posts by other teachers. These commission members have varying interests in the larger question of promoting Irish dancing, even varying notions of what Irish dancing is, depending upon their age, location, background, and experience. But it is competition that brings them together in An Coimisiún, and the proof is that the work of the commission—administering the competitive institution—is existentially divided from dancing for enjoyment:

> I'm not being critical now in this . . . we had a workshop in
> Dublin this year in January, the Irish Dancing Commission,
> about ceili dancing. And we spent ages arguing about the
> smallest little details of how this dance must be performed
> for competition. And whether the gent passes right shoulder
> to right shoulder, or left to left; and what you can do and
> what you can't do . . . That night when we got down to so-

cializing we had a ceili evening. And what we danced that night contradicted every damn thing that we set down . . . Eighty percent of the time we were not doing threes, because everybody will put little knacky little fiddly bits into their footwork, and everybody will—we have this word that we're trying to get rid of in ceili dancing, "embellishment"—well, God almighty, we put all the embellishments we wanted to, all the knacky bits, you know? We wouldn't have come within an ass's roar of a prize in a competition in which we ourselves would have been judge (Commission member, 1991).

Thus for commission members, their own view of what an Irish Dancing Commission should do and what they are actually able to accomplish is seriously affected by the forces of competition:

Not knocking competition and all that, but I still feel we have our heads buried in the sand doing these things that we haven't time to take our heads up, take a look around, say hey, man, where's this organization going? . . . (Commission member, 1991).

The Dance School
Teachers

Teachers are the bearers of tradition and occupy the central position hierarchically and horizontally in the society of Irish dancing. Vertically they are intermediary between the Commission and the students and their parents. Teachers are authenticated by An Coimisiún in the form of a T.C.R.G. (Certification from An Coimisiún that she has passed the exam and that her students, as long as she is currently registered, will be able to compete in Coimisiún events). Horizontally, dancing schools, which are the teachers' institutions, are nodes in the social network of Irish dancing. All dancers and their parents are affiliated with a school. They are able to compete at a feis or oireachtas because they are affiliated with a teacher who has her T.C.R.G..

The teacher experiences the daily push and pull of the forces of competition. It is the process that attracts and motivates students beyond the beginning lessons, it demands her serious professional involvement, and it can produce results both exhilarating and depressing. Through the ongoing involvement with parents, students, other teachers, adjudicators, and the national organization of rules-makers she must evolve a philosophy that integrates competitiveness and acceptance, work and play, business and aesthetic sense.

A school, however, is not necessarily all competition-oriented. Teachers and their schools often have interests beyond competition. Many schools put on shows for cabarets, fundraisers, local fairs, parades, and celebrations of all sorts. These are aspects of Irish dancing which are irrelevant, one might say, to the Commission's narrowly conceived purpose. Yet these activities promote Irish dancing and the schools that put them on. They create a web of relationships between the school as a local institution and the community in which it is located. Many teachers cultivate these activities as much as or more than their entries in competitive events.

Still, competitions define the style and motivate the school's students. Competitions may also define the year for many teachers and dancers (provincial championships in the fall, All-Ireland in February, World Championships at Easter). Preparation for competitions, both solo dances and group ("figure dances") require preparations in movement, costume, mental attitude, and logistical arrangements that bring parents and other assistants into a flurry of activity.

Teachers are motivated to encourage especially the better dancers. The continued involvement of a successful competitor is not only an enjoyment in and of itself for a teacher, it is also a boon to the reputation of her school. For a dancer and her parents, medals and trophies are a record of valued social distinction and cultural achievement. Yet all of these positive valuations of competition entail the negative aspects of the agonistic model, summed up in the fact that there are no winners without losers.

Dancers (and their Parents)

Children who remain in the activity beyond the beginning class repeatedly go through the structured process of being ranked with other participants, divided into winners and losers. The change in status from structural equality (contestants) to hierarchy (winners/losers) poses threats to self-esteem and to social relationships. These threats will be experienced differently by children at various ages. Young children especially are likely to experience these threats as much through interaction with their parents as they are as individual personalities. Then the developed personal skills of the parent in handling victory and defeat are relevant.

> *Catriona, age ten, danced in the Ulster Oireachtas expecting to win or place within the top three. In the competition itself one of the other girls, a very good dancer, actually fell and, as it was near the end of the music, did not continue to dance. It seemed to Catriona's parents that the fallen dancer would very likely be disqualified or ranked so low that it would make it even more likely that Catriona would win. As it turned out, the fallen dancer won the contest and Catriona came in much lower than expected. She won a medal, but was not in the top ten places.*
>
> *Catriona herself said that she wished someone would tell her what she is doing wrong that she doesn't win. She said she would rather her teacher did not tell her, "You danced beautifully; you were great," but rather tell her what she needs to do to win. Her parents thought this was a good attitude for Catriona to have. It shows a certain determination and a recognition that the teacher was only trying to keep her from feeling bad about herself, whereas Catriona was ready for more particular criticism. The teacher said that Catriona gets the requested criticism every class. She simply doesn't work hard enough to be in the top tier of dancers. The teacher also said that Catriona's personal style of dancing is very good and very musical, but that she lacks a certain athleticism that is in vogue for many judges. Therefore she would have to work extra hard to achieve that style, which does not come naturally, in order to win. Furthermore, Catriona doesn't actually take criticism very well* (Field notes, Newcastle, Co. Down, 1991).

Teachers, parents, and dancers must all three wrestle with the contradictions built into the aesthetic game. Only one can win though many may be very good and may be very good in various ways. Thus even personal styles, personal body-types, costumes, the extent to which the looks of a child match the judge's idea of beauty—all these things are subject to ranking, albeit unconsciously, by a judge selecting a winner. Catriona wants what no one can give her: a calculus for victory, so to speak: do this, this, and this, and you will win. She naively believes at this point in a complete rationalization of the aesthetic and hasn't recognized the subjective element in judging which is both essential and unpredictable.

Catriona's parents do recognize the subjective aspect of judging. However, not wanting to undermine their daughter's faith in the process they take care not to blame the judges' taste directly or too much. They want her to achieve, but perhaps more importantly to strive to achieve. Parents of course do complain about the judging, but parents who do so in front of their children—and some do—begin to inculcate a cynicism about competitions. The cynical attitude at a young age diminishes interest in competitions and perhaps in the dancing itself.

The teacher is the most adjusted to the game of Irish dancing. She knows that other forces are at work in the competition besides who dances their best, or who does exactly what their teacher tells her. At the same time, the teacher here puts the fault in two places: the dancer's long-term effort and the judges' taste in style. These are two elements that must coincide for victory. Of course victory is rare and the many disappointments call for a developed repertoire of explanations and an understanding of the attitudes that go with them. This is the larger game of Irish dancing. For example, the teacher must sort out priorities:

> Those who are going to the feis, do your best. That's all you
> can do. If you get a medal, that's great. If you don't get a medal,
> it's a pity. But if you get a medal and don't do your best, I'll
> kill you. [Smiles all around] (Teacher, Limerick, 1991)

This teacher hones in on the aspect of the competition that the dancer can control. With humor and a nod to the elements of chance, she inculcates a moral order existing outside of competition results. Children seem to take these sorts of messages well. In many cases, it is a parent who is more of a worry to the teacher: "If I find a parent is pressurizing a child. I tell them 'Leave them alone; they've only one teacher.' Sometimes it works" (Teacher, Cork, 1991).

Some teachers have told me that, when talking with parents, they take care not to fault the adjudicators' decisions even when they are obviously in error because this may give parents a bad impression of the process. Rather, they discuss the aspects of dancing on which the student must continue to work and improve. This rhetoric, of course, serves the purpose of preserving the legitimacy of the competitive process to the ones who are paying to play. And this is key: for the game to remain meaningful, the potential of fair play remains crucial. This is true within the event and in managing social relations around the issue of keeping students. Teachers may suspect that competition is a problematic force, but to keep faith in it and look for solutions to its dysfunctional effects keeps the game intact.

Competitions at younger ages in more local feiseanna are less stressful. The pressures are all there, but the stakes are low enough (often every competitor gets a medal) that parents and dancers can adjust to them with less stress. At higher levels of competition the same pressures and contradictions are more intense:

> It's not reasonable to want to win the Worlds. You have to work too hard. You have to give up everything else and dedicate yourself solely to dancing and train every day. And you have to take constant criticism. You'd want no ego, now, with your teacher. Oh no, its not reasonable at all. I wouldn't wish it for any child. At the same time, if a child wants that, I'll work with them.
>
> I asked Yvonne—she was back from *Riverdance*—did she want to give the World one more go. "No," she said, "I wouldn't put my body through that now." And I don't blame her. It's not reasonable (Teacher, Limerick, 1999).

Also at higher levels of competition, dancers are more likely to have developed relationships with other dancers outside their own school. While competition can upset relationships within a school, it may be more likely with older dancers and at larger competitions:

> Last year I was chatting away to them, you know, before the competition. And I went up. It was the first time I ever won an All-Ireland. They wouldn't talk! The same people wouldn't speak to me afterwards. They really wouldn't speak to me afterwards. And then this year, because D. won other people wouldn't talk to her. They didn't congratulate her. . . . I mean, I know her mother has influence. I know she has influence because of who she is and because of who her mother is. . . .

But that's not the girl's fault, you know? It's the judges who judge. They are the people who give the results. If you lay blame at anybody's doorstep, it's the judges'. You don't take it out on the person who won (Dancer, Cork, 1991).

This twenty-year-old dancer shows a sophisticated understanding of how social networks between various teachers/adjudicators can influence results. That understanding would be shared with many her age whether it actually accounts for a result in any given circumstance or not. It is always available as an explanation for results, albeit a cynical one. Here the dancer voices a moral point of view that puts social relationships above results. While few would disagree with the principle in the abstract, the comments she makes illustrate the pressures of the competitive process on social relations.

Some few competitors become physically ill before or during their performance on stage. Nearly all experience "nerves" in competition. Responses vary from dancer to dancer and occasion to occasion:

Because you do practice, you practice an awful lot. And I mean you can get up on the stage and you can just make a complete mess of it, even if you have practiced, and it's just because nerves get too much. . . . Yeah, I can't even explain why I love it so much, why I get such a buzz from competition. It's a huge adrenaline rush (Dancer, Galway, 1991).

For this dancer "nerves" are linked with the thrill in competition. They are inextricable. Competition produces pressure and intensity not present in other presentational frames of Irish dancing such as cabaret for tourists:

The difference between the two things is unbelievable. You're doing totally different dances, totally different atmosphere. In competition everyone is watching you. You have to be good. There's a lot of pressure. But here [in a cabaret performance], you just enjoy yourself and everyone thinks it's brilliant and everything (Dancer, Galway, 1991).

Dancers speak of the pressure to do well. Parents speak of the price of costumes, shoes, lessons, and travel.[2] Teachers talk of managing over-zealous parents, getting good effort out of students without losing the enjoyment, and keeping up on the latest steps so their students can compete. They also know that announcements in the local paper of a school's winners enhance its reputation and bring in new students. The ideal is to manage these pressures while keeping a sociable disposition. Those moments when the effects of the pressure become obvious mark the danger of competition and become the stuff of stories and talk.

The Transfer Rule

A point of articulation between teachers, parents or dancers, and An Coimisiún is the rule that applies to a student's change of schools, known as the Transfer Rule. While An Coimisiún recognizes the right of parents to choose their children's teachers, it also acknowledges the interest of the teachers in retaining children they have trained and inhibiting a free flow of students between schools. Although the rule is written with exceptions and explanations under ten headings, the heart of the rule is a limitation on the transferring student's right to compete:

> Where a pupil, formerly the pupil of a registered teacher, joins the class of another registered teacher, the new teacher must not enter that pupil in any registered competition until six calendar months following the date on which notification of the pupil joining the new class is received in writing by the Regional Council or other appropriate authority (*Rialacha An Coimisiún*).

The transfer rule thus provides a limited support to teachers' desires to retain their students. For teachers involved in the competitive aspects of Irish dancing, recruiting and keeping talented dancers is an issue, one in which the adversary can be seen as parents or other teachers.

Students are an economic resource for a teacher; they provide her with an income. A successful competitor brings attention to the school and results in increased enrollment. In the teacher's means of production, talent is the valued resource. Because the talent in this economy is located in children, parents are important players in the relations of production. Parents may very well take an interest in who teaches their child. As talent is recognized in a competitive dancer, the teacher's interest in keeping the student and a parent's possible interest in shopping around for the best teacher may come into conflict.

An editorial in *Céim,* a periodical published by An Coimisiún, in 1985 addressed this issue in particularly dramatic terms:

Some years ago, only an odd teacher was suffering from this dreaded creature, "the Poacher", but now to aid this monster, comes the over ambitious greedy parent who moves his or her child again and again from dancing school to dancing school, often inveigling others to leave as well . . . It is debatable—or maybe questionable, is a better word, to ask if World Championships have been responsible to a large extent for the desperate pressure that is being put on teachers by parents from year to year. Unfortunately it has got to be said that some teachers too are greedy for fame through results got by hook or by crook, and poach top dancers from other teachers' schools, by way of promises and criticism of other teachers thereby causing much heartache and disturbance of varied and intense degree all over the country (Níc Shim-Uí Dhálaigh 13).

The above formulation caricatures the motivations intensified by competition as immoral person-types—the greedy parent and the monstrous poaching teacher. Parents may indeed wish to move their children around in search of a teacher who somehow produces more wins for them, whether they think it is through better teaching, choreography, or even social connections and reputation. Parents may also criticize teachers fairly or unfairly and influence other parents' decisions with respect to the school their children attend. Pressures from this sort of conflict may be directly experienced through the loss of one or more talented dancers, or they may be anticipated and feared through talk, stories, and reports.

Meanwhile, the author of the editorial argues, "it is debatable—or maybe questionable" that competition is responsible for the "desperate pressure." The logic implies that, after all, competition is not responsible: people are responsible. Competition is cast as a neutral process. Rather it is people who give competition its qualities, especially fairness. What is downplayed in this formulation is precisely *the configuration of motivations* that are arranged in a particular hierarchy of importance by the competitive model. Nothing in the competitive game itself rewards loyalty of students to teachers, or refusal by one teacher to take the former student of another.

Even as the editorial places blame on immoral person-types, it recognizes the potential role of competition in creating pressure. In the organization of Irish dancing this is an issue raised by teachers. Here the authority of An Coimisiún is involved through its practice of registering and certifying teachers as authentic thus qualifying their students to compete in its sanctioned competitions. An Coimisiún resists complete identification with teachers' interests and it is this very issue over which the Comhdháil Muinteoirí na Rincí Gaelacha split away from An Coimisiún and the Gaelic League in 1969 (see Chapter Two). Because An Coimisiún frames itself as a national organization and derives its authority and authenticity from the Gaelic League, and especially because it accomplishes its mission through competitive practice, it is constrained to appeal to wider interests than just those of the teachers'.

While parents and their children gain the right to participate in this "official" competitive process through affiliation with a school, this process produces its own rewards, among them distinction and another kind of authenticity, namely victories and titles. However, such are the rewards of success in this process that the pressures to succeed may apply differentially to parents, students, and teachers. The danger for some teachers is that loyalties and other expressions of social affiliation may weaken under this pressure. These contradictory forces, stemming from the competitive institution itself, define another layer of game or competition in Irish dancing.

Competition and Choreography

The vast majority of Irish dancing teachers are former competitors and champions at one level or another. They have experienced the bodily practice of discipline and the competition for distinction. They have also experienced the development of the dance form beyond the technique required to win when they were in competitive form. The hyper-development of Irish dancing technique has outstripped most teachers' abilities to keep up. Many of them can no longer perform the competitive movements they must teach. In this they are like many athletic coaches and even closer to teachers and choreographers in aesthetic sports like figure skating.

The choreography that they develop must be a process of co-production with their better dancers. The pull of competition requires that they experiment with the movement potential of the dancer. Creative and proficient dancers invent moves and hone them under the judicious eyes of their teachers who make their own suggestions. In this exchange between dancer and teacher, new choreography emerges. And in the development of these dancers, new teachers/choreographers are trained.

Not all teachers have the talent in their dancers to produce collaborative work of a high caliber. And not all teachers are as talented in creating choreography as they are in training dancers. As the form reaches new heights of development, the roles of teacher and choreographer become more specialized. In the past decade more teachers have sought the help of better choreographers in developing material for their competitive dancers. Thus the inherent contradiction of the folk dance or national dance that only specialized professionals can perform and teach becomes more and more pronounced through the competitive process.

Adjudicators

The adjudicator is the bearer of standards in Irish dancing for the purposes of the competitive event. The adjudicator might be said to produce the event in the sense that dancers perform, but it is the adjudicator alone who turns them into winners and losers. While human adjudication is present in athletic games, the role is limited to the application of rules. The referee's or umpire's decisions can affect the results; however, in the aesthetic sport, the adjudicator's decisions are the results.[3]

Now consider that the adjudicator, a teacher herself, is situated in a web of relations with other teacher-adjudicators as well as with performers and parents. This makes every decision at once interpersonal as well as aesthetic, social as well as cultural, and intersubjective in significance no matter how subjective or objective in process:

> All that is needed is an honest opinion. If I give it [first place] to someone because I know them, it doesn't do them any good and it doesn't do me any good. (Adjudicator, Galway, 1991)

The model of modern sport requires that competitions appear to be "fair," that social affiliations do not influence results, and that officials are competent in their knowledge of the rules and, in the case of aesthetic competitions, the form. Thus the reality of the social embeddedness of the adjudicator must be, in varying contexts, submerged, denied, counter-acted, or controlled. To assist in bringing adjudication under some sort of rational control, An Coimisiún has set up rules and requirements governing the accreditation of adjudicators and the judging of competitions, as well as an appeal and review process for complaints.

A person wishing to become an adjudicator (A.D.C.R.G.) must be registered with An Coimisiún, have a teaching certificate (T.C.R.G.), be at least thirty years old, and pass an examination. The examination includes a practical test in step-dancing, written tests on Irish dance music and on "the official handbook of Irish dances" *(Ar Rinncidhe Foirne),* a practical test in the adjudication of step-dancing and ceilí dancing, and an oral Gaelic language test for those intending to adjudicate in Ireland. The practical test in adjudication takes place in the setting of a competition in which the candidate's results and comments can be compared with those of the official adjudicator. In this way An Coimisiún can evaluate the candidate's ability to produce normative results, i.e., to agree with the official adjudicator.

To further regularize the process of adjudication and make results comparable, categories of evaluation are specified with equal weightings: timing, 25%; carriage, 25%; execution, 25%; and overall impression, 25%.

> There are very basic rights and wrongs in Irish dancing. Very basic. We dance to very strict tempo music. Therefore the dancing must pay tribute to the music. It isn't like ballet where the music pays a lot of tribute to the dance. The way we do, we interpret the music, especially with hard shoes on, and even with soft shoes. But we have to interpret the rhythm of the music. So that's uppermost in every adjudicator's mind when they sit down to adjudicate.

> And following timing and rhythm, comes deportment. You may have noticed we stand very straight in Irish dancing, but not stiff. It's very difficult to create that balance in a pupil between stiff and relaxed-and-straight.

> And the next area, execution of steps: that means where the feet are placed. At all times we must have good foot placement. You know, you can't have your feet wide. You can't have your knees wide. You know, you have to have everything neat

and in order.

> And last—some people tend to stress it a little more than others these days—is appearance. I personally don't pay as much homage to appearance (Adjudicator, North America, 1988).

While the categories are universally recognized, the weightings are perhaps more theoretical in the official position. In practice, adjudicators only produce a ranking of competitors, though their comments as to faults or good points may come under these headings. It is clear from the above remarks by an adjudicator that the relative weightings of these categories may vary from one judge to another. The category of overall impression, called "appearance" by the adjudicator above, is in many ways an omnibus category that need not apply only to costume. In fact, the adjudicator quoted above continues:

> Now another area . . . the most controversial area of adjudicating that there is, and that is: Who do you think is good today? It's a personal choice and sometimes that particular area, from the general audience watching or other teachers, or the teacher of the kid that's presented, can say, "My god, that adjudicator must have been off her rocker." But then that's where that personal choice comes in. It's very difficult to say, "I like that style," and then ignore it and go for all the things you're supposed to go for. I pride myself in being able to do that (ibid.).

The defining categories (timing, execution, carriage) ultimately give way to qualities that challenge if not defy categorization. Impressions are, after all, holistic, immediate, and often ineffable. This category recognizes what everyone knows: that human aesthetic evaluation is not subject to some sort of objective control. Yet this feature is couched within a system of standards. Rational standards of adjudication are a requirement of the modern competitive model where competitions must appear to be fair. Losers want to know why they lost. They want reasons. At the same time, reasons can never fully account for the final selection and ranking. The category of overall impression indicates the hole in the dam of control. Through this hole innovations stream as adjudicators respond holistically (no pun intended) to performance impressions.

Costume and Dancing

Especially in higher levels of competition, the first three categories (timing, carriage, execution) provide ways of eliminating competitors. A questionable carriage, whether "not straight enough" or "too stiff," serves to remove a dancer from consideration, as does dancing out of time (not synchronized with the music) or poor execution (e.g., knees moving away from the sagittal plane or feet not crossed). Even one momentary lapse in any one of these categories can justify a lower mark from an adjudicator. The fourth category allows for more play including consideration of "material" (movement invention, choreography) and the controversial dimension of appearance. This is the single category in which the adjudicator may be impressed with the unexpected.

> Years ago appearance meant how you appeared or presented yourself on the stage. But these days appearance means: Do you have a really ornate costume? Sometimes it can throw you. You know, you have this thing in your mind: only the good dancers spend lots of money on Irish dancing. Not true anymore. Anybody that's interested spends lots of money on Irish dancing. And sometimes you look at a dancer that's presented to you, and they've got this ornate costume on and you think, "Oh, my god, this is my number one. This is the champion." And they fall flat on their face on timing and all the other things, you know? So, as I say, some adjudicators do tend to place too much emphasis on appearance (Adjudicator, North America, 1988).

Though this adjudicator plays down the place of costume ornateness in Irish dancing, she also reveals its effect. When the dancer in a fancy costume makes mistakes in carriage, timing, or foot placement, it is easy to see the limited effect of the costume. It is another story when such violations of the formal rules are not committed. Then the ornate costume creates the desired effect: "Oh my god, this is my number one."

The effect of costume is not lost on students, teachers, and parents watching results. The impact of the costume on results has produced a competition for impressiveness in costume design:

> We hadn't the costumes the children have [now]. I had a white plain dress with a royal blue waistcoat, a white shawl

with a hat and a shamrock. But that was the style at the time. No elaborate costumes. . . . Excuse me now, Frank, that lady's a dancing teacher. She says the costumes will be able to dance on their own soon. Fashion show! Make-up, curls, everything. They're not children anymore on the stage; they're all paint and powder! The innocence is gone (Former dancer, Limerick, 1991).

And comments from another teacher:

You know, the last few years without a doubt like, it's gone overboard now. I mean in the last year now the colors are so outrageous. I mean you'll see a costume now with three different luminous colors in the lining. I mean, O.K., one color. But now you nearly have to have three colors. Oh, I don't know. I don't know where it's all going to stop, because it's totally gone away from tradition. . . . It seems to me now it's all flash and color. (Teacher, Galway, 1991)

The development of the costume and other aspects of appearance illustrate the subtle way in which the competitive process produces change in formal features precisely through the process of adjudication. This process is anything but subtle in the long term. However, the progression is able to take place in this feis and that feis, bit by bit, even while various participants *including adjudicators* criticize the developments.

From plain dresses and simple skirts, the costume has progressed through embroidered Celtic knotwork borders, then embroidered shamrocks, Tara brooches, and Claddagh rings, to appliqué figures from the Book of Kells with satin inserts on velvet dresses with cardboard sewn into the front panels to show the design without crease, to representations of musicians, instruments and dancing shoes, to rhinestones and glittering gemstones. The development of the dresses has been paralleled by other features and accoutrements of appearance, from wigs to face sparkles:

You have to have some hair decoration. There's no way people will go up without hair decoration. It's got nothing to do with the dancing, completely ridiculous. And if you don't have the latest up-to-date costume, forget it. If you don't have false tan on your legs, if you don't have tanned legs, if you go up there with white legs, you can forget it (Dancer, Galway, 1991).

Some years ago girls started wearing tiaras in their hair and these were eventually banned by An Coimisiún. However, other hair decorations not technically tiaras but which created the effect of a tiara, came into vogue. The steeplechase for most impressive appearance finds its way around whatever obstacles An Coimisiún is able to throw up. In a sense, rules such as the tiara ban only add to the game. There has been discussion of more potential limitations imposed from the top, that is, by Coimisiún rules.

For all the criticisms about the costume and other features of appearance, there seems also to be a fascination with the development of what is referred to as "glamour" in Irish dancing and just where it all will go. Once when listening to two teachers complain about the direction and amount of change in the costumes, a woman sitting behind me tugged my sleeve and whispered in my ear, "They're just old-fashioned. I think the costumes are beautiful."

Different evaluations of the costumes may also be expressed by the same person in different situational contexts. Teachers may criticize the costumes in moments of reflection. But in practical situations of choosing a costume for a dancer or reviewing a specific performance, the same teachers may also discuss the "beauty" of this or that costume and how "gorgeous" it is. They may criticize a less ornate costume as being too old or not good enough for the dancer's talents. Teachers may choose costumes according to a logic of competition which they criticize when in a more reflective stance, for example, considering where Irish dancing has gone or will go. By the same token adjudicators reward innovators as winners in the practical role of competition judge and then lament the innovations in more abstract discussions. The competitive game shifts the concerns from any notion of preserving tradition to winning the contest. And that is largely a matter of impressing the adjudicator. This can be done with costume, hair, tanned legs, wigs, sparkles on the face, and innovations yet to be discovered.

Costume and appearance are dimensions of the form where champion-level dancers may push the limits as they do with features of the movement itself. Adjudicators, insofar as they do not specifically downgrade innovations (which may be very subtle and only one small part of an overall impression) accommodate the thrust of change in the direction of the more impressive, glamorous and, some might contend, "gaudy" costume and appearance.

The form thus continues to develop along certain lines, a progression of impressiveness. A conservative adjudicator may downgrade a competitor for one or more aspects of dancing that he or she finds "too modern." But it is very difficult to do so if that dancer also happens to be the best and most impressive in other ways. Thus something an adjudicator doesn't particularly like may still be rewarded and then imitated by others. The only way to stop the development of such features is through rules passed by An Coimisiún:

> I suppose some of the best dancers do it [a current innovation]. And they win, not because they're doing that, but because they are the best dancers. Basically everyone tries to one-up on the other person. If there's a rule, they will all be too delighted to say, "We're all under the same restrictions" (Commission member, 1991).

Even when two dancers are equal in performance, one in a fancy costume and the other in a simpler one, an adjudicator would be under a certain pressure to reward the fancy costume, precisely because the fancy costume has become normative. To deliberately select against such a costume would be a radical departure, not something judges are trained or encouraged to do by the authenticating process of An Coimisiún. After *Riverdance* there were a number of competitors who wore Riverdance-like costumes. Had adjudicators selected for them a revolution in competitive Irish dancing costumes would have occurred. But adjudicators evidently were unwilling to make that sort of departure from what has become the normal, now even traditional, competitive costume.

Social Interpretation of Adjudicators' Results

Another force of competition is the interpretation of adjudicators' decisions, regardless of how objective they try to be. Most adjudicators are also active teachers; so the situation is not uncommon where roles are reversed between two people. In effect, they are judging each other's students at different feiseanna or at the All-Ireland or World Championships:

> To keep it fair and reasonably honest—as long as you've got human beings adjudicating human beings, there's always an

element of "You pat my back and I'll pat yours." I mean I'm not going to pretend that we are all beautiful people in Irish dancing. But they're not in figure skating either. The only process we have of keeping it fair is by having a panel rather than one adjudicator for a championship event. We have an odd number. Sometimes we have five; sometimes we have seven; most times we have three. We have to have three to call it a championship. If they just danced in front of one adjudicator it would just be a competition. To have a championship it has to be three. That gives you the balance (Adjudicator, Teacher and Commission member, 1991).

Having more than one adjudicator does make it impossible for one person to absolutely determine results, especially with respect to first place due to the scoring system (discussed below). However, one adjudicator's lower mark may still make the difference between winning and not winning or, say, qualifying for the World Championship at a provincial *oireachtas* (regional competition). Thus having multiple judges does not necessarily remove the specter of non-aesthetic, specifically social, reasons for their results. The only official manner of control is through complaints to An Coimisiún. If there are a large number of complaints about a particular adjudicator they may decide to review his or her results for patterns of discrimination. Such reviews appear to be very rare.

Unofficial means of control on adjudicators' decisions include any and all means of reciprocity, including grading one's rival's students low (or high) in another competition where roles are reversed. The social entanglements of any adjudicator may always be a potential rhetoric and justification for less than pleasing results. And less than pleasing results can likewise threaten social relationships:

I told Jimmy on the phone, "You can put your sleeping bag down elsewhere!" [A reference to the fact he had given Jimmy a place to stay during local competitions in the past.] He ranked our boy fourth when the other two adjudicators gave him a first and second! (Teacher and adjudicator, 1991).

or

He's never been good to us (Teacher about an adjudicator, 1991).

In fact, an adjudicator may incur the wrath of a friend because he went out of his way to guard against a social bias. Therefore this pressure can be seen to arise from the situation, and not from the presence or absence of bias.[5] All that's needed is an honest opinion, but what is entailed may be quite a lot more.

In a championship-level competition, through which dancers can qualify for the Worlds, at least three adjudicators rank each dancer. A point system is applied to each adjudicator's results and the scores for each dancer are combined to produce the final results. Under the current system each adjudicator's first place dancer receives 100 points; second gets 75; third, 65; fourth, 60, and so on, the lower rankings being distinguished by single points. The large drop from first to second is explained in terms of a first place being "worth" so much more than a second.[6] By this logic, "first" in an adjudicator's evaluation is meant to represent something more than an ordinal value.

The scoring system has been an area of controversy and concern for An Coimisiún. Articles discussing the fairness, application, intent, and practicality of the point system and its revisions have appeared in various issues of *Céim* (nos. 8, 17, 21, 40, 42). The underlying conflict appears to be the concern for preventing the deliberate skewing of results by one adjudicator (who may or may not be attributed with intentions other than fairness), and for a system that reflects a valuation of first as significantly different to second. It has also been suggested that it is meant to reduce the possibility of ties in the first several places. Again, the logic points to the importance, even necessity, of distinction, of separating winners from losers.

The game of Irish dancing is one of social disjunction, the ritual separation of dancers into winners and losers, those who place and those who do not. While rational procedures are designed, debated, and applied to make the contests fair, at the heart of the game is the human element of evaluation and comparison. While evaluation is an integral part of artful performance, comparison is not. It is the comparison of performances that produces the results and the whole game of Irish dance contests. I would argue that this has two important results on very different analytical levels.

One result is the social and personal drama of the event where dancers, parents, and teachers experience the emotions attendant to winning and losing, and come to understand these and the whole event through participation with their cohort.[7] As dancers, teachers, and adjudicators put themselves through the excitement, drama, and effort of the feis, they accommodate themselves emotionally and cognitively to multiple themes. These range from the personal stresses of nerves and anticipation to the social means of support and empathy; from the many and myriad explanations of competition results to questions of the relation of talent and effort; from questions of access to resources (whether costumes, choreography, lessons, and all the rest) to the authenticity of Irish dancing itself. When one considers that in a contest of 50 or 150 dancers there is still only one winner, it may be that a story that makes one laugh about it all is an important balm.

The other result of the comparison feature at the heart of aesthetic competition is the narrowing and hyperbolizing of style resulting over time. The requirements of adjudication (timing, carriage, execution) produce limitations on the range of innovations. At the same time, within those limits, innovations are sought and developed that produce an ever more impressive result: higher leaps and kicks, more colorful and ornate costumes, more audible beats per bar of music, and so on. It is largely the game—the contest frame—that has shaped the form of Irish dancing over time.

CHAPTER FOUR

Learning a Body Language

In the beginners' class, where the uninitiated learn how to move in order to dance, the basic elements of the dance form are on display. To unpack what the movement means, what and how it signifies, and the range of values incorporated in this dance form one could scarcely do better than to watch and listen to a teacher work with students who know little or nothing about it. This chapter is an exploration of meaning in movement, learned with the learners.

Irish dancing is neither non-verbal behavior nor a translation of words. Dancing and spoken language interpenetrate, perhaps most clearly in the dancing class. There may be other kinds of body languages completely divorced from speech in the process of learning, evaluation, and understanding, but this is not such a form. The meaning of movement in Irish dancing can never be reduced to words though spoken language can help one understand the form just as it helps the beginner to learn to practice it.[1]

By looking at the process of learning we are able to see how the movement is taught as a system and how the movement is a system of signification. We can see how it is structured, i.e., how whole dances are made up of "steps," themselves made up of smaller entities and so on down to the smallest units that constitute the total repertoire of movements in the system that is Irish dancing. We can also see how, in the process of learning the movements, a child also learns the values, significances, and associated meanings that attach to various aspects of the activity.

What does one learn when one takes up Irish dancing? One short answer is that 1.) a dancer, out of necessity, learns a conceptual structure to organize the movement; and 2.) a dancer also learns that these movements signify, and that to perform them is to act with intention and understanding. To look at the learning process this way is to make explicit several aspects that are not necessarily in the focal awareness of the students or teachers. For them, the explicit knowledge being transmitted is the dancing itself. However, attendant to this knowledge is the tacit level of assumptions, values, and consequences that make the whole lesson sensible and imbue the movement with meaning.

One of the characteristics of this tacit knowledge is that through its multiple associations with speech, music, and social relations, it appears (becomes) "natural," i.e. just the way it is, the way it works, the way it is done. It is, then, the consideration of these relations that is extraordinary. Dancing class is where this synthesis is "naturalized" in a process of inculcation or enculturation. This may be considered on the psychological level as the acquisition of "embodied knowledge" or habit, or on the social level as the development of cultural competence. It is in the process of teaching and learning that the conceptual and practical are reshaped together through movement and other modalities including speech and music.

Lessons

A child arriving at dancing class for the first time faces the task of learning a system of movement, a form of dancing her parents and friends call "Irish dancing."[2] She sees before her a large room with places to sit around the edges, children of varying sizes and ages, and an adult or two who are obviously the authorities, the Mum, the Sister or the Father of the place. The child must find her way into this new space of people and actions. But she has help:

> The teacher comes over to greet a new student, "And who is this come down to me?" The child's mother introduces her: "Now, Mary, this is your teacher, Mrs. Lynch." An older girl, a neighbor, comes over to greet Mary. The teacher welcomes the new student, takes her by the hand, leads her away from her mother and onto the floor, the place of dancing. She is the center of attention for the moment, held on one hand by the teacher and on the other by her neighbor friend.[3]

From the very start the new corporeal experience is embedded and formed in social relationships with teacher and fellow students.[4] The new child is surrounded by friendly talk, smiles, looks, tones of voice, gestures, and movements. While all of these modalities of communication are important to a complete description of the learning experience, a look at the connection between speech and movement will suffice to demonstrate the incorporation (literally, taking into the body through control of movement) of concepts in learning to do Irish dancing.

First Moves, First Steps

Physical education in Irish dancing features verbal cues that accompany the movements. These cues are not standardized, each teacher has her own version. The spoken accompaniments function as descriptions, indices, and memory aids. In addition, the spoken phrase contains a rhythmic structure which matches that of the various dance meters: jig, reel, hornpipe and slip jig.[5] Thus the spoken accompaniment in teaching reinforces the rhythmic structure to be enacted in the danced movements. "One-two-three" is a verbal phrase describing three changes of weight that constitute a movement sequence. The movement itself goes by the name of "the threes." This sequence becomes a unit in choreography and, with appropriate changes in rhythmic expression, appears in various types of solo and social dances. It is often the first step a beginner learns, and will be analyzed in detail below.

Of course, dancers are encouraged to internalize the verbal cues that match the movements so they are not actually speaking while dancing.[6] The association, however, of words and movement at this fundamental level is one of the many reasons it makes no sense to consider Irish dancing a "non-verbal" expression. Neither should verbal cues be privileged as the defining feature of the dancing. The words used by any given teacher cannot be abstracted from the lesson and then treated as a code to the meaning of the dancing. For example, a teacher may say, "hang the leg" instead of "lift the leg." Apart from the context of the movement, these phrases may appear to mean two entirely different uses of the leg when in fact they do not.

It is precisely the use of words (along with gestures and movement) that inform the specific dance technique being learned. To put it differently, Irish dancing does not work exactly like spoken language when it comes to meaning. There is no equivalent to lexical units—words, prefixes, suffixes—that carry standard, discrete, and dictionary-like meanings. Some movement systems can and do function in this way (e.g., the sign language of the classical Indian dance form of Bharata Natyam). The use of words in Irish dancing is a matter of description, information, motivation, refinement, and comprehension of the movement, not a matter of translation. The process of teaching and learning reveals the practical-cum-conceptual connection between movement and spoken language.

The process of learning the one-two-three begins with the student holding the teacher's hand [Fig. 3], often flanked by another older or more experienced student. The teacher begins, "Now lift your right leg." [Fig. 4] The teacher and the other student demonstrate. But the child is looking around the room, distracted by the other children playing, talking, or eating candy. The teacher may tap the child's right leg. "Come now, Mary, lift the fat leg."

With very young children this teacher uses the terms, "fat and skinny," rather than "right and left" legs. She maintains that right and left have no particular meaning yet and the humor of fat/skinny gives children some way to remember that there is a difference. It is not yet crucial for the child to properly name the difference; rather it is important to get the notion to lead with this leg and then follow with the other.

3. Taking beginners by the hand. Part of the body language in learning is a matter of touch, support, leading, and literally "taking one by the hand."

When the student lifts the proper leg the teacher continues, "Now jump for one." [Fig. 5] The teacher and helper jump onto the right feet, i.e., they become airborne for a slight moment, using their left legs to push their weight off the floor, landing on the right. The student follows, or tries, and is encouraged. In whatever fashion, she is made to put her weight on the right foot. The left is now off the ground, free, not bearing weight.

The student watches the teacher's legs and feet. "Now out for two." [Fig. 6] The teacher steps forward onto the left foot, shifting her weight and leaving the right foot still on the floor where it landed. The student steps out, maybe too far, trying to match the actual distance of the teacher's step. But she is being supported by held hands and she has moved the proper foot forward.

"Good," says the teacher, "and in the back door for three." [Fig. 7] The teacher brings the right foot to close behind the left foot. "Now lift the skinny leg," and the lesson continues, the same sequence of moves, now beginning with the left leg.

Multiple Functions of Verbal Cues

The verbal cues serve a number of functions simultaneously: structuring, orienting, rhythmic, mnemonic, and semantic. The usefulness of spoken cues is, at least in part, their ability to provide a redundant method of informing the movements of the teacher and learner. This may be compared to the method of using a familiar (spoken) language to teach a foreign (spoken) language.[7] Here the familiar spoken language is used in a special way to teach an unfamiliar body language. Another option would be immersion with no resort to the familiar language, i.e., no speaking. But this is not a strategy I have witnessed in any Irish dancing classes.

Cues name the moves and, in the process, create entities, units of movement. This is a structuring function. All the minor movements that are necessary to "lift the leg" (shifting of weight from both feet to one, raising the thigh by coordinating muscles and flexion at the hip, knee, and so on) are all put together into one movement, one action.[8] Naming it reinforces the structuring process. The conceptual organization of movement into units makes it possible to build further strings of movement, and even higher-level units, by simply arranging these units in a sequence.

The structuring function allows the dancer to ignore all the minor

4. Learning the threes. "Now lift your right leg."

5. Learning the threes. "Now jump for one." The position achieved at the end of the movement is a jump from the left foot, forward onto the right foot.

6. Learning the threes. "Now out for two." Weight is evenly distributed on both feet at the end of the movement.

7. Learning the threes. "In the back door for three." The position of the dancer at the end of the movement is a shifting of the weight forward over the left foot while the right foot closes behind and crossed to the left to take equal weight.

anatomical movements that make the act of "lifting the leg" an exact replica of the teacher's act (except for instances when a teacher makes a stylistic correction—usually later in the learning process). These minor movements can recede from focal awareness and allow the dancer to concentrate on higher levels of organizing movement, for example, combining the leg gesture ("lift the leg") with the aerial transfer of weight ("jump for one") into another unit ("one" of the "one-two-three"). Verbal cues assist this structuring process throughout the learning process and reflect the compression of knowledge as the dancer learns higher and higher levels of movement organization within the system. [Fig. 8]

The verbal cues assist the dancer to orient her movements in space and time. The spatial and orientational directives and metaphors in the verbal cues all help the beginning dancer to incorporate a conception of her body as a moving center, unlike the center of, say, the room which remains stationary. "Out" means away from the body center, "in" means toward the center line (vertical, horizontal, or sagittal axis, depending on context) or center point (point of convergence of 3 axes). [Fig. 9] Initially, directional cues are not oriented to the room nor to geographical space as

Verbal Cues

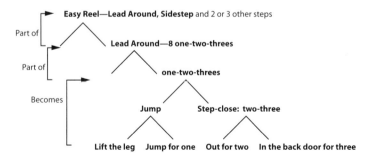

(Anatomical level of description: minor movements)

8. Verbal Cues. Structuring function of verbal cues: they reflect the structuring of smaller movement units into larger ones. The particular cues used in the first lessons may eventually be forgotten as the dancer focuses on higher levels of combination. The cues shown here are particular to one school.

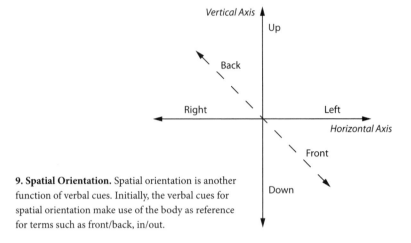

9. Spatial Orientation. Spatial orientation is another function of verbal cues. Initially, the verbal cues for spatial orientation make use of the body as reference for terms such as front/back, in/out.

they might be in some other systems of movement.[9] They make sense in relation and reference to the dancer's body. Thus, "front" is the body's front, "back," the back of the body. "In the back door" means toward the dancer ("in") and from behind ("back").

The words "one," "two," and "three," associated as they are here with movements, cue the sequential order of the movements. In addition, the spoken cues can reinforce the rhythm of the moves. For the dancer, developing conceptions of timing and rhythm are aided by accompanying verbal cues, especially the manner in which the cues are spoken with pauses, stresses, and intonation.[10] Here the spoken cues have an iconic relationship with the movement, that is, they reflect, in their timing, the timing of the movements [Fig. 10].

The verbal cues function as mnemonics. As the lesson is repeated again and again the separate actions begin to go together with each other and with the cues. The student can be reminded of the movement simply by saying the words. Some students write down the verbal cues to whole dances to help them remember sequences.

The verbal cues also link the spatial, temporal, and bodily aspects of the movement system to various values and meanings in the larger culture and society. For example, the metaphor of the dancer's body space as a house ("in the back door") is rich, entailing notions of boundedness, a separation of inside/outside, invisibility/visibility, private/public. In the

1-2-3

10. Musical notation for the threes in reel time.

dance lesson, these metaphors are rarely expanded upon or explicated. They simply appear and make sense in the context of the lesson.

Especially with young children, the teacher may use story-like language because she feels it will help them remember what might otherwise appear to be unmotivated sequences of movements. By informing the movement with meaning and motivation, the teacher helps the child turn raw movements into actions, that is, intended movements:

> *Come here, now, I want to tell you a story. Who watches Bosco on TV? [Bosca, Gaelic for 'box', is a children's television show. The main character (Bosco) lives in a box (Bosca).] It's my favorite show. Now, where does he live? . . . And how does he come into his house? That's right, he comes in the back door. Now, let's do the one-two-three like Bosco. Sneak in the back door to Bosco's house.*

The "story" is created by this teacher using the shared resource of children's television programming. The repertoire of concepts and their use in the dance lesson must make sense. The meaning that develops for the children and the teacher is only partially to be found in the surface story that has the television character, "Bosco" (the trailing foot), "coming in the back door" (toward the center point below the center of weight). The deeper meaning for the movement system is the sense of "in" versus "out," and "front" versus "back."

These spatial referents are deep, because they are never *merely* directions; they are always unavoidably associated with cultural meanings and values. That is to say these directions and relationships signify. The back door is not the same as the front door. They have different functions, different meanings. For example, the back door is less public. Bosco "sneaks" in the back door. These nuances of meaning, associated with front and back of a house, are associated with the body in the dance lesson through the cues, as the body is metaphorically made into the house of the story. Thus the direction in which a dancer faces, and how the trailing foot returns to its position under the center of gravity, makes a difference, it signifies. The front of the body is for presentation—to the audience, evaluator, adjudicator. The movement that brings the trailing foot below the center of gravity is not emphasized as presentational.

These connections between movement and spoken language, between movement and other semiotic systems (architecture, clothing, music), between movement and culture, reconstructed in dance class, are always inextricably practical and conceptual. In the process of teaching and learning, the doing of the movement can simply not be separated from attitudes about how it should be done, from ideas about what the moving is like, from feelings regarding the social relationship between teacher and student, from notions of success and failure, good and bad, better and worse. All of these attitudes, ideas, feelings, notions, and ideals are constantly instantiated in looks, touch, and speech, but never more clearly than when the teacher is making corrections and working on the style with which movements are performed.[11]

Style: How Steps are Performed

> *"The teacher says to me, "It's how you do the step. Any fool can teach the step."*

Dancing is not simply a matter of body mechanics. Dancing is about the proper conception of the movement that makes it possible for the dancer to do it well. Teaching and learning are cognitive exercises filled with explanation, value, a sense of right and wrong, good and bad, what must be done and what must be avoided. Meaning, sense, and the prescribed movement are co-present in the teacher's words and actions:

> *"Ready? Back the shoulders. Back the hands. Now try and watch your leader, and don't be making mistakes, right?" Twenty-three girls and two boys form up one behind another in five lines facing the teacher who bends over the tape recorder ready to start the tape of a lively reel. Their hands are at their sides, the right leg extended, and toes pointing forward low in*

preparation. Each line is led by one of the more accomplished dancers. The dancers know the sequence of steps. All of them have been through the repetitions at slow speed. Some of them have been dancing the Easy Reel for a couple of years. The teacher expects more from them than simply remembering the sequence. These dancers are working on the manner in which they perform the steps: they are working on style.

The single most noticeable feature in the style of Irish dancing is the contrast between the upper and lower halves of the dancing body. The upper half is relatively immobile, the lower half moves with extraordinary verve—leaping, hopping, jumping, twisting, sometimes making audible rhythms on the floor and always creating visual rhythms. "Carriage" is the held position of the upper body: torso held extended in place high, shoulders held back, and arms held down at the side. [Fig. 11] The challenge to students in learning this carriage is to hold these body parts in these positions while executing the steps with the legs. Normal use of the upper body to balance and provide counterweight to movements of the lower limbs has to be transformed. The dancer has to retrain her body, strengthening key muscle groups, in order to maintain the posture while moving. This lesson in physical control is a hard one, and one that takes years of practice for most students of Irish dancing:

The teacher places the students with their backs to a wall to induce an image of the ideal posture. "Push your shoulders and head back until they're touching the wall. Keep them there. Arms down at the side. Now step out away from the wall. This is good carriage. Relax now, not stiff." But the little girls are tense through the upper body as they try to hold that position along with the mental image of their backs straight as if against a wall. They embody the discipline, if crudely, and only imperfectly.

Most beginning level students have trouble maintaining the posture. The torso tends to incline forward during forward leaps to counterbalance the legs. The arms tend to come out or up also for the sake of balance. For many dancers, even some very good ones, the look of stiffness will never leave them. Others, some of the very best, will learn to maintain that posture and will look, if not quite relaxed, at least not stiff. Yet, as

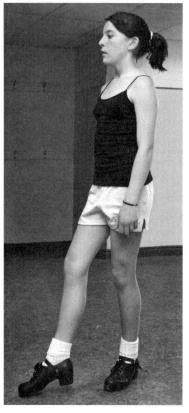

11. Posture in Irish dancing. The posture in Irish dancing is held throughout the dance, including difficult jumps and leg gestures.

they keep at it (ever reminded by the teacher to keep straight), arms down, shoulders back, and "back the hands" (as a way of keeping the shoulders back), they gain more and more control and approach the ideal carriage for Irish dancing.

An extraordinary amount of physical control is built into the ideal execution of Irish dancing. The posture is an extreme example of physical discipline and control in the form. For the dancer learning the proper style of Irish dancing, there is no question of why it is so. It simply *is* the form of Irish dancing that must be learned. And here is the meaning of discipline in this form, that authority is accepted ("This is what you do") and responsibility for control of one's body in the prescribed manner is internalized ("This is what I must do"). To the extent that the student attempts to work on control of her body or displays such control, she manifests discipline and merits reward.

Irish dancing particularly emphasizes the vertical dimension, *the* dimension treated by Lakoff and Johnson in their "Orientational Metaphors" (14-21). The up/down duality maps many value-laden oppositions that apply to other Irish (and not specifically Irish) ideas as well. Happiness, consciousness, health and life, having control, goodness, and virtue are all associated with "up." Sadness, sickness and death, unconsciousness, being subject to control, badness, and depravity are all "down."

When the dancer moves through space it is not only physical but cultural space that is navigated. Several of these oppositions map easily onto the Irish dancing body, divided as it is at the waist, stillness above and movement below.

Emphasis on the vertical axis, and especially the "up" value of the duality, is established by the held position of the upper body. While dancers gesture with their legs in the sagittal plane and, to a much lesser degree (feet only), in the horizontal plane, the torso, head, and arms always stay upright on the vertical axis. This emphasis is reinforced by aspects of style in the lower half of the body mainly through extension, dancing on the balls or toes of the feet, as well as keeping the knees together and feet crossed: *"This is the most important thing. You mustn't let the knees go out. Glue your knees together. Pull up in the knees."*

There is a turn-out of the feet in Irish dancing, but unlike ballet it does not originate in the hips as much as it does in the ankles.[12] The knees are kept as close together as possible.

> *The teacher ties a sweater around her assistant's knees and has her walk along a line, pointing her toes with each step, to demonstrate and evoke an image to help the students incorporate the lesson, "as if you only had one knee," she says.*

Crossing the knees and feet is also a feature of the style, referred to as "execution" or "placement" in the context of judging. It is as if the lower limbs take their place in the sagittal plane rather than the vertical plane. In reducing the body's occupation of the vertical plane the appearance, from in front of a dancer, approaches that of a vertical axis, at least for the lower half of the body.

The ideal form of Irish dancing, especially for girls in the light shoe dances, approaches dancing on point as in ballet. Of course, Irish dancing is not done in point shoes so this is nearly impossible except in hard shoes where the fiberglass piece on the ball of the foot can reinforce a brief toe stand [Fig. 12]. Nonetheless, students are often reminded to dance up on their toes and many can accomplish a 1/2 toe and some can stand on 3/4 toe in soft shoes. In order to accomplish this, dancers have to force the arch of the foot, extending the ankle as much as possible while the weight is carried on the pads of toes and ball of the foot. The foot is supposed to retain the extension whether weight is on it or not.[13] In leg gestures the

12. Toe Stand. The fiber-glass taps covering the toe on the sole of the shoe provide the reinforcement necessary to support this position.

13. Kick behind. The one-two-three with posture and gestures that are recognized as "good style". The accompanying photo illustrates a "kick behind."

toes are required to be in the same line as the lower limb: *"It's a sin to have your toes up. You have to stiffen the toe and squeeze."*

The language of discipline here indexes a whole cosmological and moral system of belief (sin/grace) institutionalized in a social system of authority—the Church. It is a language and reference the children know well, not that they necessarily take the reference seriously. They have, to varying degrees, become acquainted with the teacher's sense of humor, but neither is the force of the metaphor lost:

> *The teacher manipulates a girl's toes and foot to show how they should point. "Ow," she complains. "The reason you're saying 'ow' is you never point your toe!" It is hard work developing muscle and tendon strength as well as flexibility in the ankle to keep the toes "pointed." The teacher has the students walk on a line, as if on a tightrope, as far up on their toes as they are able. This exercise combines the style features of keeping the proximity of the knees and feet to the sagittal plane and the extension of the foot while moving the lower limbs.*

Another feature of style in executing the one-two-three is an added gesture during the aerial portion of the jump. The leg from which the jump begins, i.e., the take-off leg, does a "kick behind" [Fig. 13]. It is a quick gesture that appears to assist the lift the dancer achieves in the jump. The whole gesture takes place in the vertical and sagittal dimensions. These are the two dimensions in which most of the movements are defined.

The jump requires flexion of the weight-bearing leg before and after the aerial, otherwise the idea is to dance as high up as possible on the toes with the whole leg extended. The jump is made only minimally forward; thus the vertical is emphasized over the sagittal. As the "up" value is emphasized in the vertical duality, the "forward" is emphasized in the sagittal.[14] The dancer's step on the "two" is a step "out" which the teacher encourages students to take with as full an extension of the stepping leg as possible. Moving through this step-out, forward and high, to the dancer's count "three" in full extension is a feat of power, of strength:

> *"Come on MOVE! Push your legs. Do you know what 'jiz' is?" asks the teacher. "It means lifting the legs. I want you to dance with jiz." The teacher uses this word for a sense of energy, spirit, life, and speed.*

Class Atmosphere and Work Ethic

In addition to body positioning, Irish dancing style is a matter of effort, a display of energy manifesting in vertical leaps, quickness, sharpness, and power. Getting children to put this effort into their dancing throughout the course of the lesson requires techniques of motivation:

> *"Up on your toes. Now, Maeve, you have to start dancing up on your toes." It seems to me that Maeve will never get up on her toes. She doesn't do it easily, or one might say "naturally," nor does she seem to have great drive to work at it. The teacher ties another child's shoes for the eleventh time since class began forty minutes ago. "Now let's see, Maeve, are you going to dance up on your toes?" The class does one step and stops. "OK, next step." Maeve wanders back to sit next to me and when the teacher calls her up to dance, Maeve whispers to her. "Did you hear that?" says the teacher. "She has to save her energy for her first confession tonight!"*

The teacher is a mixture of humorist, drill master, nurturer, comforter, cajoler and more. She takes no breaks for herself, though class is often interrupted with shoe-tying, spill-cleaning, comforting hurt feelings, and a hundred and one other things. There is work going on in this class, but the atmosphere is also relaxed and social. After a fifteen to thirty minute stretch of dancing, the more advanced students will be allowed to take a break while the teacher works more directly with newer students.

Despite the resistance in some of these young bodies to incorporating all the elements of style in a very difficult dance form, the teacher persists. The first time the teacher brought me to her classes she introduced me as a professor of Irish dancing from America come to evaluate their progress. Then she told me with a smile, "You have to play all kinds of tricks on them." The teacher and her assistants chuckled at how this would tame the unruly and put all on their best behavior. It worked. Children asked how many marks they had accumulated. "Did you look at me?" asked a little girl. Teachers often use whatever is handy and whatever they can create to motivate their students. The promise or threat of evaluation is common:

> *Standing next to me with my notebook and pen she announces, "We're writing down all the names of the foot floppers. We're*

Figure 14. On the sidelines of the class. Break time between dances, a time to chat and snack.

> *writing down the names of all those who don't know where*
> *their toes are." My notebook and pen are again in the service of*
> *motivating the students.*

Evaluation is an ongoing aspect of learning in this pedagogical model and it is also an integral aspect of performance.[15] At least one dimension of learning a performing art, such as dancing, is to put oneself in the position of being evaluated "for the relative skill and effectiveness of the performer's display of competence" (Bauman 11): *"Let's see who can place their feet the best. Michelle gets the highest marks from the adjudicator. I know who has the second highest. (A chorus of voices) Who? Who? Who"?*

The language of competition in class is accompanied by many small competitions with prizes such as the leading place in a line of dancers, the right to sit down first to one's snack, positive recognition by the teacher, and on rare occasions, candy. Evaluation in the frame of competition is the game of Irish dancing beyond the beginning class level. Students who respond well to this type of motivational device may very well move up to competitive levels of dancing. Teachers are always on the lookout for recruiting better performers for competition.

For historical reasons, competition is integral to the practice of Irish dancing. Consequently it is a prime motivating factor even in a beginning class. But there are exceptions. Motivation is not always framed in the model of competition. Individual improvement is also sought and rewarded regardless of a student's comparative competence with respect to other students. Once working with a boy who was having trouble pointing his toe, the teacher manipulated his foot into the position desired. She called over his older sister and told her what she wanted him to work on. The teacher then told the boy he would earn 50p if he came back able to "push the toe out." The boy began to improve immediately in class. He began to work at it.

The Class Feis
As an activity, Irish dancing is a physical discipline, but one that is about performance, presentation, evaluation. That is, it is an art form even at the beginning level. Students in a dancing school may take an exam once a year and take part in a class or school feis once or twice a year. In an exam, each child is simply graded; it is not a competition. A class feis, however, is conducted in the manner of a formal competition with an adjudicator, stage, audience of parents and family members, and medals, but may utilize taped music rather than hired musicians.

The class feis is a presentation of the school to the parents who pay for their children's lessons; it is a presentation of Irish dancing; and it is a social occasion for children, friends, and neighbors. Most importantly, it is a presentation of self for each dancer in and through the medium of a performance tradition. A tradition with roots in a national past thus indicates one dimension of the dancer's identity. It is the presentation of self in dancing that most informs the event for all assembled. Each child is groomed and dressed in her or his best. Those who own Irish dancing costumes and shoes wear them. Those who don't wear their Sunday best:

> Three at a time the children are called out to perform the Easy Reel. The first three form a line upstage center and face stage left where the teacher is announcing their names and the dance. [Fig. 15] Also located stage left are the tape player and an assistant who recites the verbal cue-accompaniment to the steps. This helps put the dancers at ease and, hopefully, makes it unnecessary for them to recite as they dance. The teacher takes care to put one of the more accomplished dancers first in

*line so the others can follow her lead, just as in class. The first
three do well. They dance the lead-around making a circle once
on the stage and then face the audience to execute the sidestep.
At the end of the five steps they dance the lead-around again
and face front to bow to the adjudicator and audience. The second three start well but must be stopped after the lead-around
to reorient one of the very little dancers. She has begun to execute the sidestep facing stage left, where her teacher is, where
the music is, the way she has always performed the step in class,
i.e., facing teacher and music. She is learning now that the
stage is different from the class. Although the teacher is there on
the side of the stage, it is the adjudicator and the audience
whom she must face. This reorientation in space takes some
time. An assistant has to help the little one face front for the
sidestep. Now she seems to understand.*

Several of the performances are interrupted for this sort of lesson in
the semantics of stage space or for the tying of shoes. Children are coached
in taking a bow after their Easy Reel. After the entire class has danced
both reel and slip jig, results are announced often with two-, three-, and
four-way ties for the first three places. Every child receives at least hon-
orable mention and a medal.

The experience is positive and celebratory and at the same time parents see what their children have learned and accomplished, and what
they have not, relative to other children. Many are happy to see their children dance on stage at all. One very little girl, aged three, began crying as
she was brought to the stage. To dance on stage is, first of all, a display
and this is said to require confidence. Her *de facto* veto indicated that she
had not yet the confidence to perform in this formal setting. Confidence
is evident in the fact of performance and is considered a great asset. To
have danced on stage, even if with relatively little skill, is still an accom-
plishment.

In addition to being the culminating event of a series of lessons, the
class feis is also the doorway to more competitive levels of Irish dancing,
for the transition from one level to the next hinges on the parental support and interest in precisely this type of event. Parents may or may not
explicitly evaluate their own children with respect to the relative skill and

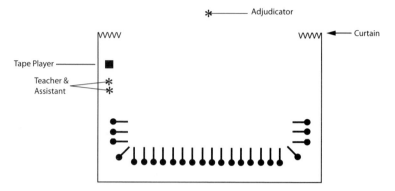

Audience

Figure 15. Staging the class feis.

effectiveness with which they danced the movements; however, it is very difficult not to get drawn into the game of comparing dancers and choosing one's own winners and runners-up. This is precisely the game of aesthetic competition and the role of the adjudicator. To the extent that parents get pleasure out of this aspect of the experience, and especially in consideration of where their child places in the ranking, they may become interested in further competitions. Sometimes it is a parent who becomes hooked on the competition and drives the child.

Values: Physical and Social

In addition to the values associated with the body, space, and movement itself (front vs. back, up/down, the posture, etc.), there are generalized values associated with the whole activity of Irish dancing. Whatever parents think about competition, the value of the dancing as physical-social education at the beginning level is nearly universally recognized. The following statement by a teacher of Irish dancing encapsulates the range of values typically associated with the form as an education in physical culture:

> Organised movement must be concentrated on co-ordination exercises in order that we learn more control over the various parts of our bodies . . . to develop the habit of good posture which can mean a healthy body for life . . . to create

an impression of vitality, confidence and attractiveness. . . . It is my firm belief that Irish dance is one of the greatest forms of development any child can partake in (Carty 5-6).

Three dimensions to this notion of physical education stand out. First, there is concern with the development of the body as an organism that must be maintained and strengthened via exercise. There are many activities available that can provide this benefit including sports, other types of dancing, and informal play. The choice of Irish dancing for one's child may not be based on this dimension of the activity, yet its inclusion is invariably cited as positive. Furthermore, some, including the teacher cited above, contend that the posture of Irish dancing is itself conducive to good health, that it aids the structural development of the body.

Second, there is concern with the person's developing ability to control his or her body, that is, to effect a kind of bodily discipline. This dimension of physical education involves both the neuromuscular and social-cultural coordination of body use. In practice, the coordination of body movement with an external motivation such as a measured beat is inseparable from the coordination of body movement with cultural mores. Both are learned simultaneously.

A child learns certain body techniques at the same time he or she is learning that the process itself is positively valued by others. Discipline is expressed as a value, and this means both learning to learn and learning to control. Furthermore, the movement system the child learns instantiates values such as good posture. Good posture is not qualified by "for this dance form" or "for the coordination of these movements"; it is simply "good." The benefit of good posture may apply to either the body-as-organism or the culturally-embodied person. This combination of the physical and moral in bodily control is summarized in the term "comportment," or "bearing."

Third, there is concern with the development of positive appearances. This dimension specifically involves the social level of physical culture through presentation. The teacher's statement above recognizes that organized movement creates "an impression" of vitality, confidence, and attractiveness. As we saw in the class feis, it is not only the movement but the context of presentation in which children are dressed and groomed their best that highlights the importance of creating a good impression.

The presentational dimension of Irish dancing separates it from other kinds of physical education.

The fact that Irish dancing is a performance art is also central to its value for parents and children. In the Irish cultural setting, expressive form is highly valued. While not everyone can be highly skilled in music, poetry, dancing, or storytelling, everyone is encouraged to have something to contribute to an evening's entertainment. Everyone should have their "party piece." Glassie points out this feature with respect to the céilí in Co. Fermanagh (*Passing the Time* 99-100). This can be generalized to many Irish settings. An instance of this cultural value can be seen in an Irish television program titled "Party Piece" that aired during 1991. It was a children's program consisting of various performances of music, song, recitations, dance, jokes, and stories in pairs, in groups or solo, by each of the children in a school class selected for the show. The program featured a different group each week. The exchange of roles—now performers and now audience for each other—recapitulates the ethos of shared responsibility for entertainment at a party.

The performance aspect of the physical education in Irish dancing is not restricted to formal presentations. In a sense the individual is always involved in a presentation of self, a physical performance of self. As we see above with the value of positive appearances, physical education in Irish dancing is believed to enhance one's social standing. Teaching manners continues in the modern dance teacher's role, much the same as in the dancing master's role in the seventeenth and eighteenth centuries.

When the teacher greets the new student and leads her onto the floor to teach her Irish dancing, she begins a process of physical, moral, social, and aesthetic education. The focal point of this education is the control of one's body in the technique of Irish dancing. This is the normative level of Irish dancing, where the principles and movements are only at issue for the child who must learn to master them.

If the child continues with Irish dancing, she and her teacher may begin to create movements, floor patterns, and sequences. This is the experience and process of Irish dancing beyond the normative level. This is the collective process of representation where new expression is negotiated, selected, or eventually rejected, and variously interpreted.

Creativity and adaptation is a use of this open system that, as we have seen, is already dense with signification built in from the first steps, through the development of style to performance situations. In the process of creativity, the movement system is explored to find new possibilities of expression. Meaning, however, is never a simple and uncontested matter. Therefore, with new moves and new dances come also new struggles over interpretation, meaning, and significance.

CHAPTER FIVE

Creativity, Form, and Identity

The elaborate development of Irish dancing, perhaps in contrast to many other folk or national dance forms, is a result of a century of creativity powered by competition. Creativity is an important and defining part of the overall practice of Irish dancing.[1] Yet there are rules and restrictions at work in this dance form, tied to the notion of tradition.[2] In order to create within the idiom, and in the process to further shape the dance form, the rules and restrictions—the grammar—must be mastered. Highly skilled play with the form of Irish dancing thus reinforces, even as it challenges and changes, aspects of the form. And change it does. As the form changes, questions about its identity inevitably arise.

Broadly speaking, there are two kinds of creativity in dance forms that we can distinguish: 1.) reordering existing movement units; and 2.) introducing new movement units.[3] The first kind is much more common in all sorts of creativity, as well as in Irish dancing. The second kind is not only more rare, but also more uncertain in that it is a gamble in terms of how the new movement communicates, whether it will be accepted, and whether it will pose a threat to currently accepted relationships of signs in the system and even to the identity of the system itself.

Both kinds of creativity are to be found in Irish dancing. The second type will be discussed with respect to three movements introduced to Irish dancing in the late 1980s. The composition of new dances via the ordering of movement units is itself a very complex and fruitful arena for creating new effect. One reason is that because dancing consists of the moving body in time and space, each of these dimensions provides means by which movements can be differently aligned, that is, shaped, formed, and put into context. In other words, a simple 1-2-3 can be differently placed in a dance relative to: 1.) other body movements; 2.) timing, or the rhythm of the music; and 3.) orientation or room space. This complexity in dancing provides for endless variation and elaboration, the nature of which we can begin to see by comparing two dances.

Analysis of Two Slip Jigs: Beginner's and Champion's
Comparison of a beginner's dance and a champion's dance illustrates the modes of invention possible within the form as prescribed by its defining restrictions.[4] This analysis explores features of choreography, or what Irish dancers refer to as "material." In a championship level contest one needs both good material and flawless execution. At the beginning level many students will learn the same dance. A beginner's dance is not personalized to feature the strengths of a particular performer as would likely be the case for the highly competitive dancer. A champion's slip jig is one that very few, if any, other dancers would know. The champion's dance featured in this comparison was choreographed by the dancer herself and her teacher. Both of them have a strong preference for inventing rhythmic variations. Comparison with another champion's dance will reveal slightly different information regarding aspects of creativity. One dancer may play with gestural sequencing while another dancer might focus more on rhythmic variation. However, both champions will play with both dimensions, rhythmic and gestural, much more than a beginner.

The comparison is only carried out for the first four bars of the dances because there is so much information regarding body movement, use of space, and timing—the three analytical sections that follow—that this will suffice to illustrate the ways in which dancers create within the form. The Labanotation script for the first four bars of the two dances [Fig. 16] can give, even to the novice reader, a sense of the difference in complexity.

Body Movement
Body movement, here analytically separated from uses of space or time, consists in combinations of weight changes (steps) and leg gestures (kicks), together called moves.[5] Weight changes include jumps and hops. These smaller moves are organized into motifs, each of which is indicated in Figure 16 by a large parenthesis and its name represented in small brackets, e.g., {UUD}. We begin with a comparison of the smaller moves.

Figure 16 shows that there is little repetition in the champion's dance as compared with the beginner's. This can be gleaned by the repeat signs in bars two and three of the beginner's dance.

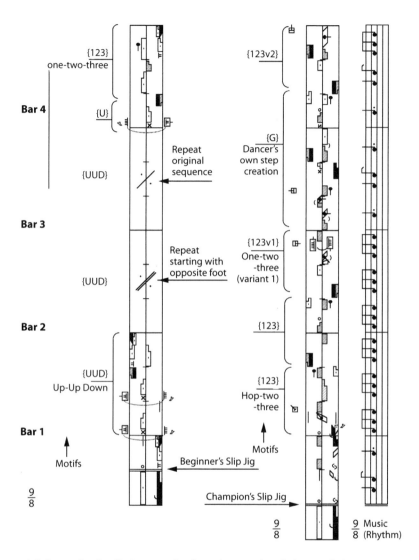

16. Labanotation for slip jigs. First four bars of Beginner's and Champion's slip jig.

The beginner's dance uses three moves [Fig. 17]. Two moves are used repeatedly in the first three bars while the last bar has all three moves (hop/cut, jump/kick, and step-close or "two-three"). Counting each repetition, there are twelve moves in the beginner's dance. This total is close

	Beginner's Slip Jig		Champion's Slip Jig	
	Moves	Number of times performed	Moves	Number of times performed
1	Jump/kickB	4	Jump/kickFB	3
2	Hop/cut	7	Jump/kickF	1
3	step-close	1	Hop/cut	1
4			step-close	3
5			step-pivot	3
6			step-pvt-close	1
7			step-level-change	1
8			Jump/touch	1
	Total moves	**12**		**14**

17. Comparison of beginner and champion movements. Moves used in first 4 bars of two slip jigs and number of repetitions each.

to the champion's dance (14 total moves). The champion, however, uses eight different moves, five of which are not repeated at all in this sequence.

Unvaried repetition is not found in the champion's dance. The beginner's dance repeats the movement of the first bar in the second and third, though on alternating feet. The fourth bar begins the same as the other three, but ends differently. The differences between these passages are that the champion adds turns, pivots, and level changes to the jump, hop, and step-close.

At a higher level of structure (motif level, several moves = one motif) some repetition can be seen in the champion's dance. In fact, the first two bars of the champion's dance consist of three variations on the "one-two-three" ({123} = a motif, described in the last chapter). There is one more variation on the {123} in the fourth bar of the champion's dance. The intervening motif ({G}—a long, low forward gesture with the right leg followed by a step onto the toe with a left leg kick behind) is made up of similar moves, but these are in a different sequence for rhythmic and spatial effect.

None of the movements in the champion's dance, considered alone, are particularly difficult to perform for one trained in Irish dancing. The difficulty comes with the complexity of the order of moves, including variety in rhythmic alignment and use of space. Execution of moves while maintaining features of style (e.g., posture and extension) is a challenge to both beginner and champion; however, it is obviously more of a challenge when the sequence contains fewer simple repetitions.

Time: Rhythmic Stess

Normally, in musical terminology, only the first note of each bar is referred to as the strong or primary beat. To analyze the rhythmic complexities of this dance, I have found it necessary to consider that 9/8 jig meter provides three strong beats per bar. Each of these strong beats is the first of an eighth-note triplet. The second note of each triplet is a weak or unstressed beat, and the third note is a secondary beat not stressed as much as the first note of the triplet but more than the weak beat [Fig. 18].

All weight changes in the beginner's dance fall on the strong beats with one exception in the fourth bar [Fig. 19], which falls on the secondary beat before the third triplet. The steps of the dance thus fall throughout this passage, with one exception, on the strong beats. In addition, three of four gestures in each bar fall (i.e., reach their positional destination) on the strong beats. Only the upper leg gesture to forward middle

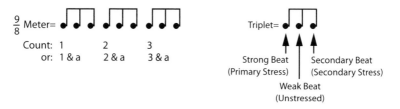

18. Rhythmic structure of slip jig meter. (Numerals = primary beats; & = weak beat; a = secondary beat.)

19. Rhythmic structgure of beginner's dance. Rhythmic alignment of gestures, steps, and path segments. (Numerals = primary beats, & = weak beats, a= secondary beats.)

occurs on another beat and it, like the weight-change exception, aligns with a secondary stress. The champion's slip jig brings out all three subdivisions of the beat. Weight changes fall on the primary and secondary beats [Fig. 20]. The secondary beat, however, is emphasized slightly more. There are eleven changes of weight occuring on the secondary beat while only nine occur on the primary beat.

Gestures in the champion's dance fall on all three subdivisions of the beat. Of the twelve gestures, seven fall on the weak beat, four on the primary beat, and one on the secondary. Figure 21 shows the alignment of weight changes and gestures with subdivisions of the beat in the first four bars of both dances. Clearly the competitive dance brings out or exploits the metric subtleties of the slip jig musical form more than the beginner's dance.

Rhythm is, of course, a more complex concept than meter. Meter is simply a regular repeating pattern of stresses. While any such repeating pattern may be considered a rhythm, it is of the most basic kind. More complex rhythms, while based on a pattern of repeating stresses (which may be assumed rather than counted out or otherwise made audible) such as the meter of a musical piece, deviate from this straight expression of the pattern to play with various kinds of emphasis, elision, and re-

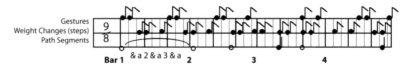

20. Rhythmic structure of champion's dance. Rhythmic alignment of gestures, steps, and path segments. (Numerals = primary beats; & = weak beats; a = secondary beats.)

Movement/Beat	Beginner's Slip Jig	Champion's Slip Jig
Weight/Primary	12	8
Weight/Weak	0	0
Weight/Secondary	1	10
Gesture/Primary	12	4
Gesture/Weak	0	7
Gesture/Secondary	4	1
Total Primary	24	12
Total Weak	0	7
Total Secondary	5	11

21. **Comparison of beginner and champion rhythm.** Comparison of body movement with subdivisions of the beat.

structuring of the pattern in terms of sound or movement. A good example of this more sophisticated rhythmic variation can be seen in the champion's slip jig.

The repeated motifs, variations on the {123}, in the first two bars of the dance are structurally similar with respect to time. The aerial move (jump or hop) takes one triplet and the step-close or other finishing move takes another. But rather than aligning these motifs with the same beats of the measure, the advanced dancer places them in three different positions in the measure. In fact, the very first beat of the dance begins with an aerial. The second aerial occurs on the third beat of the first bar and the third occurs on the second beat of the second bar. Thus the rhythm of the step brings out three different emphases in two bars of music. If we consider the aerial portion of the motif to be the emphasis—as we might from the value given to lightness in the slip jig and the vertical dimension generally—then the emphases of the three motifs are not directly aligned with the musically stressed beat (first beat of each bar), but hit the first stressed beat and frame the second [Fig. 22]. Alternating strong beats (dancer's

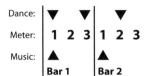

22. Aerial stresses. Aerial stresses (▼) in the first two bars of the dance create a polyrhythm of 3/2 with stresses in musical meter (▲) on the first beat of each bar.

strong beats, 3 per bar) are emphasized, creating a short polyrhythmic pattern of three stresses in the dancing over two stresses in the music.

The aerial portions of the motifs are also marked by gestures that align with the emphasized strong beat. These are followed by quick gestures on the weak beat. These leg gestures emphasize both the aerial quality of the motifs as well as the strong and the immediately following weak beats of the triplets on which they occur [Fig. 23A]. The weight changes mark a different set of stresses [Fig. 23B].

Together, gestural and weight-bearing movements create a visual and kinesthetic rhythm. Their rhythmic emphases are differently structured but create a complementary set of patterns in these two bars [Fig. 23C].

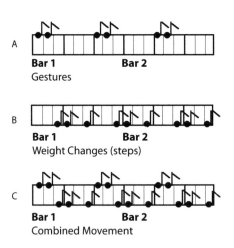

23. Rhythmic alignment. Alignment of gestures and weight changes with musical meter, creating polyrhythm.

Space

There are two kinds of space relevant to this analysis, one nested in the other [Fig. 24]. Body space is the sphere surrounding the body through which all parts can move individually or in combination. This may be considered gestural space. This space is located within coordinate space, here related to rooms, such as a stage or dance studio. This is the space through which the dancer moves on a path or track. Semantic considerations (meaning and intention) determine the various kinds of space suitable for analysis. In some movement systems, for example, geographic or astronomical coordinates are relevant (Williams, "Role of Movement"). In Irish dancing the competitive stage, with adjudicator/audience implied, provides the relevant coordinates.

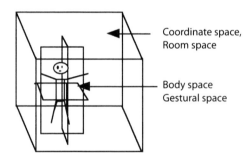

Coordinate space, Room space

Body space
Gestural space

24. Body Space. Two kinds of space: body space within coordinate space.

Orientation or facing is also relevant because of the adjudicator/audience. As the dancing body is always upright in the stage space and there is no head movement in competitive Irish step-dancing, orientation here means the direction in which the whole front of the body is aligned or is facing.

The use of coordinate space has a temporal aspect. It continues the organization of movement by creating, in effect, another rhythmic level or shell within which the rhythmic uses of the body in body space are embedded. For example, the polyrhythmic aerial sequence analyzed in Figure 25 is united by one path segment and separated from the next sequence by a change in orientation (she turns from facing downstage left to face stage right). The change in path actually follows the last aerial gesture while the steps complete the rhythmic pattern:

The beginner's track is an even half-circle throughout the first four

Gestures
Weight Changes (steps)
Path Segments

Combined Movement with Path Segments ◄— Change in direction

25. Rhythmic pattern of champion dance. Rhythmic pattern of first two bars of the champion's slip jig, incorporating spatial element of path and path change.

bars [Fig. 26]. The repetition on the moves and motif levels are mirrored in the floor path. The one deviation from the repeating pattern marks the halfway point; the second four bars of this dance complete the circular path. The champion's floor path consists in three distinct lines of direction which also combine and separate motifs in this passage.

While both choreographies make use of the path to further structure the motifs, it is a more complex relationship in the competitive dance. The first straight line path holds together the first three motifs with the third step-close variation producing a change in direction. The {G} motif, however, is divided into two path lines by a 180-degree turn. This dramatic change of direction takes place during the simplest rhythmic and non-gestural passage, thus adding an emphasis in path complimentary to the quietness, so to speak, of the body movement. It precedes and contrasts with the focal gesture-step sequence of {G} (the long, low forward gesture followed by a step and quick kick behind) which is set up for max-

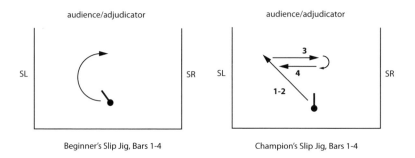

26. Floor paths. Track data of beginner's and competitive slip jigs, first four bars. SR=Stage Right.

imum viewing effect, i.e., it "reads" best from a side view. Here, the spatial aspect of the choreography has less to do with the temporal or rhythmic structuring and more to do with the semantics of stage space.

The path of the beginner's dance describes a circle that takes the dancer, her orientation to the path remaining constant, through half the possible facings with respect to the horizon of the room. However, the four sides of the room are not equivalent; one side, the front, is more important because of the performance/competitive framework centered in evaluation and a critical point-of-view. Judges sit facing the front of the stage. Perhaps more accurately, the location of the judge (or other authority, e.g., the teacher in the classroom) determines the front. The relation between body space and room space is informed by this model of events even when the performance is not in a competition. From this perspective we can see that the confusion the beginning dancer experiences in facing "forward" on stage for the first time at the class feis (instead of facing her teacher on the side of the stage, Chapter Four) is as much a matter of learning hierarchies of authority in varying contexts as it is "stage directions."

The more competitive dance does not give equal time, as it were, to all facings. The champion's first path brings her forward but also on a diagonal that allows more of the gestures, all of which occur in the sagittal plane, to be seen to greater advantage. The second and third paths are toward the sides (SR and SL). This orientation of the dancer, side to the audience, allows the viewer to get the maximum effect of the gesture-step combination. The use of spatial orientation in the champion's dance is thus more varied and more presentational, aimed at showing various aspects of the choreography to best advantage.

The champion's first four bars move constantly and divide almost evenly between facing Front and facing Side (SR and SL). She has not yet stopped to dance in one location, but she has covered a fair amount of stage space. Most, if not all, Irish step-dances feature portions of the dance where performers are not moving along a path, but dance in one location. Often this is near the Front of the stage and nearly always facing Front. This feature of Irish dancing is not brought out by these four bar phrases. However, the movement around the room (path) in these passages represents a development of modern Irish dancing where stages and dance studios have replaced the unhinged door on the kitchen floor as the performance site of the form. Once, it is said, this kind of path through space was not a part of Irish dancing. Indeed some contemporary old-style (sean-nós) dancers perform whole dances in one spot.[6]

As previously noted (Chapter Four), the use of body space in Irish dancing not only tends to emphasize the vertical and sagittal dimensions but tends also to favor the up and forward values of these dimensions. The competitive dance stresses these more than the beginner's in several ways. Forward is emphasized by the replacement of the flexed gesture with extension of the whole leg forward in the jump. Also some steps taken forward are larger. Up is emphasized in the more competitive dance by, for example, aerials which remain airborne for two sub-beats as opposed to those in the beginner's dance which are aloft for one sub-beat.

Play with Form

The poetics of movement in Irish dancing mainly involve variation and dynamic alignment of movement units in the metered time and proscenium-defined space of the dancing. The variety in the champion's body movement may be located more specifically at the level of moves where pivots, turns, level changes, as well as added gestures of the lower legs, increase the bodily-spatial dynamics of the movement. Furthermore, this variety is made to stand out through a principle of contrast.

While the beginner's dance is aimed at helping the dancer learn to incorporate the rules of form through repetition and simplicity, the champion's dance is aimed at demonstrating the complexity of movement possible within the rules. The structural complexity of the champion's dance is visible, for example, in the subdivision of the beat with both gestures and steps, in the rhythmic relationship between gestures and steps, in the polyrhythmic placing of the first three jumps against the musical emphases, and the organization of movement motifs with spatial features such as path and orientation. The simultaneity of these forms of play makes the form impressive when well-crafted while the means of play in the form allow for an infinite variety of constructions.

Creativity in Irish dancing is guided by selections of movements which emphasize values already inherent in the form. Movements that bring out verticality and "up-ness" or gestures and paths in the forward direction instantiate these values. At the same time, one has to go down to rise up, move backward to set off the value of forward. Thus values incorporate their opposites. And creativity in Irish dance choreography often brings out its values through structured contrasts. A sequence along a path is set off by another in one location. A complex rhythmic passage stands out in contrast to one that features the simple meter of the music.

In a very broad sense, an aesthetic of impressiveness guides the choice of one sequence over another, one juxtaposition of sequences over another. The point is to be seen and remembered, to make an impression.

Creativity and Identity

New movements, often elaborations of accepted movements, sometimes produce the desired effect in competition, drawing attention to the dancer and providing a winning edge of impressiveness over other competitors. This is where choreographers and competitors can exercise and attain a certain creative authority. That is, they not only partake in the institutional authority that confers on them this certificate or that prize but they shape the form of Irish dancing in the process. Yet these same elaborations may provoke a controversy about the movement itself, and specifically its place in the system and the meanings of the system as Irish dancing. This issue is typically raised through the denial of identity, "That's not Irish dancing." If this is the view of the adjudicator on the day, a new movement could be the downfall of a competitor.

Sometimes innovative steps that are accepted by adjudicators remain controversial even though they are immediately copied, adopted, and become widespread among practitioners at the competitive level. Toe stands, heel clicks, and butterflies are names of movements that came into Irish dancing in the late 1980s. Each of these movements fits the prescribed canons of the form yet raises questions for the system as a symbol of Irishness, a representation of national identity.

Toe Stands

A movement called "toe stand" [Fig. 27] consists of either: 1.) a momentary freezing of movement in a completely extended, vertical position, weight borne on the point of the toes ("full toe," Hutchinson 207); or 2.)

a change of weight onto either foot where the weight is borne on the point of the toes.[7]

There is nothing in either variation of the toe stand that is outside the limits of Irish dancing defined by selection of moving body parts or the way they may be moved (i.e., the restrictions inherent in the prescriptive categories of judging: carriage, timing, and execution). It is simply an extension of the ankle joint and toes, common to gestures, but not previously used in weight-bearing steps. The emphasis on Up in the vertical dimension entails the desire to dance as far up on the toes as possible. The logical extension of this value is to dance en pointe. But this is precisely where the problem enters. A la pointe is a ballet term and refers to a defining feature of ballet dancing. The toe stand is not traditional to Irish dancing, and it is traditional to the ballet, with its own social and cultural identity (Kealiinohomoku). As a result, the toe stand raises for some people the question of cultural borrowing: are dancers borrowing from forms that are not indigenous in order to develop the form of Irish dancing? It is the semantic link of this movement/position with another dance form, possibly implying issues of cultural affiliations, which made it controversial in Irish dancing.

The referential link between toe stands and ballet could be created by viewers and not intended by the creator of toe stands, but intention, here, is beside the point. The reference is entirely available through obvious formal similarities. It is an iconic relation: they look alike. We might ask what makes this reference salient when other possible semantic links with other forms are ignored. I think we can credit the newness of the step and the familiarity of ballet, which is also taught and performed in Ireland.[8] An innovative action sign calls attention to itself and its place in relation to other present signs. With the passage of time, this connection and its attendant controversy have receded. At the time when this movement entered the repertoire of champion dancers, however, there were two reactions to the innovation: "That's not Irish dancing," a spoken criticism by whoever is concerned with changes in the form at the time; and "That's now Irish dancing," the argument of the dancer performing the movement in a contest.

One hears "That's not Irish dancing" as a critique of a step, a posture, a gesture, even a costume, or a tempo of music. Interestingly one doesn't hear "That's now Irish dancing." This is a proposition I have translated to spoken language, because it really only exists as an assertion in movement. And it is verified only in the competitive process. Movements adopted into the system achieve their authenticity from the competitive process. So the argument, "That's now Irish dancing" doesn't have to be vocalized; it simply is a fact resulting from adjudicators' decisions. What is now Irish dancing is the argument waged in terms of movement in the court of dance contests.

The controversy over innovations may highlight a fault line in the social relations of cultural production and, to some extent, be a matter of tension between generations, or those actively involved in creative choreography and those who are no longer so occupied:

> Now it's a terrible difficult thing to say, as was put to me by one of my pupils, "So … you have a right to change and modernize things in your day, but I don't have the right to do it now? So what gave you the right?" You know? Who's the one who's got to say, "This far shalt thou go and no farther. It was OK for me to modernize, but now you're gone a bit too far"?
> (Former Teacher, Cork 1988)

Since a majority of adjudicators accepted the toe stand, one might think this type of discussion moot. This is not necessarily the case. Because the adjudicators, as well as teachers and dancers, participate in an institutionalized framework of competition there are possibilities of recourse through rules to limit the elaborations of the dance form. Such was the case with heel clicks, another movement innovation that raised questions of authenticity in several ways.

Heel Clicks

> A lot of it, the treble clicks and the double clicks, I believe are not sort of Irish. What happened was the introduction of fiberglass, you see... [Formerly,] they had only leather shoes and when they went up for a click, if they got that out you'd hear a sort of "wow" from the audience. A fabulous click there, you know. Because you only dared do so many clicks. But then came the advent of fiberglass heels and, of course, rub fiberglass heels off each other and you get a fabulous clicking sound, somewhat artificial and all that, but a fabulous clicking sound and easy to get out. And so it became so easy, dancers began to experiment with it left, right and center. And then, of course, following that was "Oh, you can do two of them," you know. And then we got to the stage when dancers are now able to do three of them. And I believe some of them have actually perfected four of them. But in order to perfect three and four, you're going into the realms of full-time professional training in dancing. . . . I think at that stage you're going out of the realms of Irish dancing. (Commission member, Cork, 1991)

It is clear that shoe technology played a role in making multiple heel clicks possible. It is not that they could not have been executed with leather heels but that they would not have been as audible, as the force required to make leather heels sound is far greater. Thus clicks were limited to one per gesture by the shoe materials. Change in shoe design has become a topic of debate in Irish dancing precisely because such changes allow further elaboration which may or may not be acceptable depending on one's point-of-view and place in the social relations of the practice. Shoe technology continues to be an area of controversy.[9]

The other issue raised above is the amount of training required by some contemporary movement innovations. The heel clicks can also stand for the increasing "professionalization" of competitive dancers—not that competitions are becoming commercial in any way but that the sheer amount of training required for modern competitions brings the status of the form as a "folk dance" into question. Again, it is an identity issue.

It is not so much a question of whether or not it is a folk dance (whatever that means) but more an issue of change beyond recognition from the personal point of view of experience. Whatever terms are used, the underlying argument is something like, "We never did that. That's not the same thing." In other forms of dancing, say modern dance, this may not be a problem. However, because it is labeled *Irish* dance, some stability of form and meaning is implied. The change beyond recognition is typically felt by older participants.

In 1987 multiple heel clicks were limited by an official ruling of the Irish Dancing Commission. While double heel clicks are allowed, they may occur only in isolation. As a series in succession, double clicks are not allowed. No triple clicks nor multiples of a higher order are allowed. Along with this ruling came the following wording from the Commission: "Teachers when composing steps are urged to include traditional foot movement such as cross keys, drums, boxes and rocks" (Commission Circular).

The fact of institutional control in Irish dancing provides an interesting dimension to the forces of competition but it raises another issue, well articulated by the same Commission member above (Cork, 1991):

> [This] is a thorny one because it's not just the clicks, it's the whole question as to know: do we have the right to legislate, to limit, the extent to which the art of Irish dance is going to evolve, you know? It's evolving. It's changing. . . . I mean I know that I myself was suspended as a dancer by the [local] Teachers Association because as a pupil they said what I was doing was too revolutionary, wasn't Irish dancing. Now the particular dance that I was doing then, if you taught them to the beginners now today, they would look at you and sort of say, "Do you think I'm going to do that simple stuff?"

Complexity itself is a value in the competitive aesthetic and continues to shift the standard of competence in the form. This provides the authorities charged with the legislation of competitive rules with a conundrum:

How can Irish dancing be preserved when the very mechanism that keeps it going, lively, and interesting, i.e., competition, causes it to change?

The Butterfly

The "Butterfly" was created by a contemporary teacher and choreographer, Marie Duffy.[10] As she explained it to me, she utilized a traditional step called the "cross key" and simply placed it in a jump. Thus it combines two very traditional aspects of Irish dancing, a received traditional step, specifically mentioned by the Commission for teachers to use in composing steps (Commission circular, ibid.), and an emphasis on the vertical dimension through aerial movements. The result however was a spectacular step never seen before. It contravened no rules or tendencies in Irish dancing, but its technical difficulty and visual appeal produced an immediate impact. Many dancers copied the step, executing it as closely as possible to what they had seen. It immediately entered the vocabulary of championship dancing, and variations on it proliferated.

The interesting aspect of this creation and its reception is that the choreographer intended the movement to incorporate traditional elements, but the effect was nonetheless new and seen by some as explicitly non-traditional, even borrowed from ballet. The point is that change, which may appear to disregard tradition, can enter the form not from subversive intent but from the very desire to preserve and extend traditional moves.

The questions of identity and change revolve around two arguments, "professionalism" and cultural borrowing. The toe stand points to ballet and the heel clicks require extensive training. The butterfly indexes both arguments.[11] Technique which requires extensive training apparently contradicts the idea of dancing as an expression of a simple, rural people, the overriding image of an authentic Irish past. In this image, dancing is a "natural" activity of people who "work the land." Working at bodily expression may invoke notions of specialization via the division of labor and other modern developments which everywhere loom as replacements of a romantic past.[12]

Because toe stands, heel clicks, and butterflies require intensive training, they can symbolize the level of artful body technique that Irish dancing has attained. Also, by extension, they can symbolize the requisite lessons, expensive costumes, hair styling, jewelry, artificial leg tanning and other developments prompted by the competitive process. These developments are also available to either of the two interpretations: "That's *not* Irish dance;" or "That's *now* Irish dance."

Poetics of Movement and the Identity of Form

> "Rules that remain rules are insupportable ... Every rule is at the same time a source of deviation. The rules themselves take on meaning" (Jakobson 1969, cited in Reisman 456).

Meaning is always a matter of form and context. Movements take their unique sense from their place in relation to other structural units and levels. Sometimes a danced movement will raise an issue of identity at the level of the genre, Irish dancing itself. Although toe stands and butterflies do not violate the grammar of the form as a system of movement, by making an iconic link with semantic domains of other human movement systems, these new movements raise the issue of their place in Irish dancing. On the other hand, they challenge the conception of Irish dancing as a static tradition. This is the "not/now" interpretive divide.

This is also a matter of rules and structural relations. We might spell it out by saying there is a rule at the level of the genre (of the nationalist form) that whatever other rules operate at lower levels, the resulting movement should be distinctive to this genre, i.e., not "borrowed." Then we can see that this rule must become a matter of deviation and play, providing at least dual interpretations regarding authenticity. The rule itself is brought into relief, its meaning exposed and challenged. The other ruling concept, that folk or national dances are supposed to be simple enough for widespread participation, is also brought into relief, challenged by the technical achievements motivated by competition.

There is general agreement among practitioners that Irish dancing cannot, nor should, remain static. However, the pace of change, its direction (e.g., increasing technical difficulty), or the fact that it may include cultural borrowings all raise the authenticity question. At another level, dancers in Ireland may be concerned that North American, English, or Australian dancers are gaining increased control over the form and its development. The themes of authority, authenticity, and control thus remain, at every level, a matter of issues, struggles, and contests which begin in the dancers' body movements and extend through the adjudicators who select winning form and the teachers who teach and choreograph it, to the commission members who attempt to act as trustees of the form.

The point is not that some people are open to change while others are not, though this may appear to describe the situation at any given time or on a particular issue. Rather it is the structural relations of competitive practice and national representation that make these issues endemic. In this game, one is bound to find oneself now on one side, now on the other side of the authenticity issue with a specific movement, costume, musical or other feature of the whole form and practice.

The very structure and practice of the form, labeled as Irish and performed in competition, build in the twin notions of identity and change in such a way that they are always in meaningful relations of antithesis. In a very important sense, dancers and teachers are forced to be innovative with the formal features of the movement system. They are pushed by the competitive model to come up with new sequences of movement, new arrangements of movement in space and time, occasionally new movements themselves. At the practical crux of this antithesis, which is always already a semantic crux as well, dancers create, recreate, shape, and re-shape their own identities as Irish and as dancers—they play with the very rules that say they must be different from other dance genres, that Irish culture does not borrow from other forms, that it is unique, that Irishness itself is somehow prescribed and unchanging.

CHAPTER SIX

Riverdance: Beyond Nationalism

Two watershed events mark the history of Irish dancing in the twentieth century. The founding of the Irish Dancing Commission in 1930 was the first, for this marks the divide between diffused and centralized authority, and between informal and institutionalized competitions. Prior to the founding of An Coimisiún le Rincí Gaelacha there were locally differentiated styles. In this period the significance of the dancing may have been multi-faceted, as it is today, but it is not clear that national identity was a key feature. In fact, this seems to have been a result of Gaelic League programs. After 1930 competitions were codified and regulated under a hierarchically organized social institution with one level of meaning supplied: *this is a representation of Irishness.* The second watershed event was *Riverdance* in 1994 in which, through the power of the media, Irish dancing exceeded the control of institutionalized competitions and found a place in the world of commercial theater.[1] While it was still a representation of Irishness, the value or quality of that meaning shifted due to the new context.

Now that the century has turned and Irish dance shows continue to tour, proliferate, and occupy a more or less established place in theatrical dance, it may be possible to assess the appropriation, growth, and development of this form of expression in general historical perspective and ask some questions that relate to the past, present, and future of Irish dancing. How did it come to be as it is? How has it changed and not changed? What forces work to limit or to accelerate change? What relative places do competitive and commercial Irish dance occupy?

The Century of Irish Dance

If Irish step-dancing is an embodied argument about Irish identity in danced movement, it has been until recently a very limited engagement and a narrow discussion. It is limited by the parochial nature of its competitions. The Gaelic League successfully called attention to step-dancing as a feature of Irish culture. However, as the century progressed from the first Gaelic League feis in 1899 and the appearance of nationalist books on Irish dancing in 1902, the practice became more insular under the auspices of the Irish Dancing Commission. Contests in dancing were separated from others in Irish music, speech, drama, and so forth. The dancing became its own closed world in many ways, hidden behind the doors of the feis, to be seen by the public only at an Irish Night cabaret or St. Patrick's Day parade.

Why did this happen? The reasons for the particular approach of the Gaelic League's Coimisiún Na Rinnce—the model of social control—are not yet clear.[2] It is most likely that it is not a simple story nor that all agreed to the manner of its operation. It is apparent, however, that what ultimately became the modus operandi of the Gaelic League, the Coimisiún Na Rinnce, and later An Coimisiún le Rincí Gaelacha, was based on a certain model of authority having much in common with that of the Church and the Victorian sports league. It was deemed necessary to have an organization that would control the activity, establish a single body of knowledge (superseding the many knowledgeable bodies already dancing) and specify a certification procedure for conferring authority and authenticity within the institution. This was to be a matter of social control because it was not just contests that must be brought under its auspices but also the affiliation of individuals practicing the activity. Rather than allowing anyone at all to compete in its competitions, participants had to be officially registered with teachers, themselves officially registered with An Coimisiún.

Rules included precise knowledge that had to be held by teachers and adjudicators, a dogma of Irish dancing. Certain dances, indeed certain versions of dances, formed the canon while others were excluded. Rancorous debate surrounded the arguments on what was—or was going to be—Irish dancing (Brennan 39-43). Once the assumption was accepted that exclusion was necessary, the struggle concerned which varieties would be favored in the creation of what might be called the new "standard dialect" of the Irish dancing body language.

A completely practical reason required this dogma: competitions had to be judged. Standards had to be rationalized if for no other reason than that disappointed competitors had to be convinced that there were standards and not just prejudices at work in the judging. This practical matter had perhaps to remain in the background while, on the assumption that there was a definable "Irish" dance, self-appointed experts were allowed to legitimate both their control and specification of the form (Brennan ibid.).

The achievement of the Gaelic League was significant. It won the day. It accomplished with the dancing what it could not accomplish with the language, that is, it fashioned a standard dialect of Irish dancing and continued to exert control over it for much of the century. It must also be recognized, however, that this was an hegemony. In other words, enough people in the dancing world, especially teachers, were convinced of the legitimacy or saw the advantages of the whole enterprise to make it work. By the time of the split of An Comhdháil from An Coimisiún, the model of hierarchy, dogma, and the institution of social control over the dancing had been accepted. An Comhdháil and other breakaways reproduced the same structure. By making the dancing both competitive and institutional, the Gaelic League took it from its informal context of practice, inherently inclusive and admitting of many centers of authority—what we might call talent or performative authority—and answering to many varieties of standards.

In addition to being an achievement, it was a politicizing and exclusionary change. The Gaelic League subordinated dancing to national representation and tied it to a political agenda. At first this was a matter of distinction and independence from England and English culture. After independence was won, it was a matter of continued association with the political culture of romantic nationalism. In excluding other popular forms from the national designation, such as the sets, it may have had the unintended consequence of pushing its chosen forms out of the mainstream.

Other factors contributed to the marginalization of Irish dancing. Perhaps chief among these was the growing popularity of other forms of dance that were specifically denigrated by the Catholic Church. The Fianna Fáil government, in its own blend of romantic nationalism and Church solicitousness, passed the Public Dance Halls Act of 1935. This act required all dances to be licensed, effectively ending house dances.

The sheer enjoyment of the foxtrot and other popular jazz dance forms, as well as the waltz and ballroom dances, may or may not have displaced Irish ceili dancing as entertainment. But they certainly provided options. The reaction of the Church and government to these phenomena had an additional effect on Irish dancing (both step and ceili), pushing it into the corner of a putative moral high ground:

> In a pastoral letter of 1924 . . . Cardinal Logue distinguished Irish dancing from modern dancing: "it is no small commendation of Irish dances that they cannot be danced for long hours. That, however, is not their chief merit. And while it is not part of our business to condemn any decent dance, Irish dances are not to be put out of the place that is their due in any educational establishment that is under our care. They may not be the fashion in London and Paris. They should be the fashion in Ireland. Irish dances do not make degenerates" (O'Toole, "Unsuitables" 147).

The fusion of cultural and moral purity had an unintended consequence for the dance forms themselves. While the Cardinal may have been heaping praise in the best way he knew, the result was that Irish dancing was placed in opposition to what was popular and made to carry additional significance that is not at all clearly warranted. Writing on "The Dance Halls" in 1941, Flann O'Brien could caricature ceili dancing as impersonal and at the same time criticize the notion that it was religiously and politically safe. Yet the play of contrasts reflects the status of Irish dancing on the margins of popular entertainment as well as its identity with Catholic nationalism:

> It is a very far cry from the multiple adhesion of enchanted country stomachs in a twilight of coloured bulbs to the impersonal free-for-all of a clattering reel. Irish dancing is emotionally cold, unromantic and always well-lighted. . . . Some district judges . . . want Irish dancing and plenty of it, even at the most monster 'gala dance.' They believe that Satan with all his guile is baffled by a four-hand reel and cannot make head or tail of the Rakes of Mallow. I do not think that there is any real ground for regarding Irish dancing as a sovereign spiritual and nationalistic prophylactic (O'Brien 51-52).

For the step-dancing, gender identity became another issue in participation. For reasons not yet clear, the activity was mostly male at the turn of the century, at least teachers (dancing masters) being mostly male, but became mostly female thereafter. Perhaps the institutionalization of the dancing as an activity gave it a status equivalent in some ways to a sport, but because it was open to girls, unlike hurling or football, dancing became the province of females.[3] We can only speculate at this point, but the spurious identity of the kilt as traditional Irish dancing dress by Gaelic League enthusiasts may have played a role. By the time of Frank McCourt's childhood, circa 1940, it was evidently established that a boy dances only at risk to his gendered social standing:

> He wants to know why I'm dancing, that everyone knows dancing is a sissy thing and I'll wind up like Cyril Benson wearing a kilt and medals and dancing all over with girls. He says the next thing I'll be sitting in the kitchen knitting socks. He says dancing will destroy me and I won't be fit to play any kind of football, soccer, rugby or Gaelic football itself because the dancing teaches you to run like a sissy and everyone will laugh (143).

This attitude had not much changed by the nineties when one mother, expressing a rather common sensibility, told me she wouldn't have her son in Irish dancing unless he was also in something like football "to rough him up." This view is not however unique to Irish dancing and may be found in many western cultures of the twentieth century. Exceptions such as breakdancing are rarely taught in studios and are more exclusively male in participation and thus identity. Though Irish dancing in competitive practice has remained an activity dominated by girls, there have always been boys who have braved the taunts of peers, persisted in dancing, and achieved acclaim locally, regionally, and now even internationally. Boys who dance do apparently have the additional burden of proving their masculinity either in direct confrontations or by also participating in sport—witness Michael Flatley, touted as a boxer. This only reiterates the extent to which the step-dancing became a girl's world, somewhat closing it off from half the population of Irish children.

If still a very closed activity, it remained strong throughout the century. The folk revival of the sixties and seventies in some ways was irrelevant to

Irish dancing because it was neither in need of revival nor the preoccupation of the politically dispossessed as may have been the case with the sets and sean-nós dancing. Its almost exclusively competitive nature distinguished it from other "folk" forms.[4] In fact it was more likely seen by culture brokers of the folk revival as a spurious tradition precisely because of its institutionalized competitions. Yet as folk dance revivals in other parts of the world produced national dance troupes, several Irish dancing schools began performing at international folk festivals, representing the performance tradition of dance accompanying Irish music. Apart from these performances, however, Irish dancing remained a closed world of teachers, competitors, and their families. And in this sealed milieu the dance form developed according to its own logic of distinction and impressiveness. It flourished and spread through Irish communities of the diaspora, England, Scotland, the USA, Canada, Australia, New Zealand, and lately South Africa. In 1969 An Coimisiún established the annual World Championships of Irish Dancing (Oireachtas Rinnce Na Cruinne), recognizing the growing international participation in the activity.

Even with growing numbers and geographical diffusion, it was not a well-known art form. The increasingly specialized costume, not to mention the developing technique, made it more and more the activity of a specialized group of people, unlike Irish music or song that was shared much more widely and informally. Irish step-dancing on the eve of Riverdance was in some ways unknown in Ireland itself, or known only as a spurious tradition, though practiced avidly by those who taught and competed beyond beginning levels.

Riverdance

"They left Eurovision audiences reeling. Now the world seems their oyster"—Banner for *Irish Times* article "When Irish went flamenco," 05 May 1994.

Riverdance was a pop-cultural phenomenon in the sense that it appeared to a wide public apparently out of nowhere. The public had few preconceptions regarding the form, function, or significance of Irish dancing. They were told the dance was "Irish" and "traditional", and they could recognize it as "Celtic", a popular contemporary category of white European alternative to Anglo, carrying additional significance as mysterious, spiritual, holistic, and communitarian (Wilkinson 2003). It was also a commercial theatrical phenomenon. Not only did it become a success as a theatrical show and spawn other shows as well as another genre of Irish dance show (the arena show, *Lord of the Dance*), but it also changed the environment of international dance theater. Less than a year after its appearance as a short interlude in the 1994 Eurovision song contest, *Riverdance* was made into a full-length theatrical show and has been touring the World (Europe, North America, Australia, South Africa, Japan, etc.) with a minimum of two touring casts. In March of 2005 the tenth anniversary of the show was celebrated. By that time it had been seen by some eighteen million people in thirty countries spread across four continents.[5] *Riverdance* has already established the Irish dance show as a genre of theater in its own right, and a model for other folk and national dance groups around the world.[6]

Thus *Riverdance* has had a tremendous effect on the place of Irish dancing in the larger social context. At the same time, *Riverdance* and its progeny have had no effect on competitive Irish dancing, that is, the theatrical versions have not changed the actual form of the dance in competitions. Michael Flatley may have moved his arms in *Riverdance,* but the arms still remain at the sides in competition. Gillian Norris may have bent her torso and moved her hips in *Lord of the Dance,* portraying the evil temptress, Morrighan—Cardinal Logue's sensibilities live on—but the competitive version remains faithfully straight and still of torso and hip. Costumes modeled on the theatrical shows were tried, but they have not caught on at feiseanna. They have not been voted for by judges. So in this material and significant way the influence between theater and competition has been one way; theatrical "Irish dancing" has appropriated the competitive version, but competitive dancing has taken very little in return. On the other hand, the opportunities for Irish dancers after and beyond competition have mushroomed.

International Participation

Irish dancing was an international phenomenon from the start. The first ceili was held in London in 1897. One of the first books on Irish dancing was first published in London in 1902. It was the London branch of the Gaelic League that took an early interest in the forms of dancing, researching, constructing, and defining the parallel form of ceili dancing to the sets of quadrilles. Cullinane has shown that Irish dancing in the diaspora goes back to the turn of the century and beyond. The Irish Dancing Commission eventually took an interest in certifying teachers in foreign lands, but in some places the similar organizing efforts concerning the regulating of contests had already occurred, for example, in Australia (Cullinane, *Aspects of History* 100). In many ways it may have been easier to recognize Irish forms in a foreign setting than at home.

The existence of Irish dancing in international settings is simply not in question. It has a long history in America (Cullinane, *Aspects North America* 1991). The fact that two Americans could star in a production that presented the form to a huge international audience is really not at all surprising given this history. Still there was a process of reckoning involved between the Irish dancing authorities at home and abroad. And in some ways, Michael Flatley's career is a token of that process. Until he won the World Championships in 1975, no American dancer had won the title:

> But I remember being in the Mansion House when he won the World. Yes, and he was the first American to win it . . . And there was great jubilation. Every American teacher was pleased for him and pleased for his teacher. I remember saying, "This is a breakthrough, this is great." "That showed 'em", kind of, you know. But there had been an awful lot of good American dancers (Teacher, Adjudicator, Commission member, Ireland).

Whatever made it possible for Flatley to win, certainly his talent, but also an element of timing—"There had been an awful lot of good American dancers"—Irish dancing became more international on that day, and on the day an Australian won and earlier when an English dancer won. To recognize an American as the best Irish dancer (in his age group) was to separate the nation from a requirement of residence and a local process of enculturation. This was apparently not a step easily or lightly taken.

In the seventy years after its foundation the Irish Dancing Commission came to recognize its international basis by first certifying foreign teachers and adjudicators, then affiliating with national councils or other organizations of teachers, then allowing them representation on the Commission and, most powerfully in symbolic terms, by instituting the World

Championships of Irish Dancing.[7] However, there is a formal and informal side to each of these steps. Allowing representation is a step toward sharing power but it was in no way an equal sharing. In that sense, the foreign representatives joined the other peripheries of Ireland, perhaps even more politically distant from the Dublin center of Commission power. Starting the World Championships did not guarantee all competitors an equal chance. Flatley's win as much as any other event conveniently signals the internationalization of Irish dance, though still very much a national symbol. However, *Riverdance* marks a change in the way the national symbol itself is viewed. By placing it in a different context, he and the other creators, including Jean Butler, choreographer Mavis Ascot, and the score of Dublin dancers who performed the role of the powerful corps, created a new set of relations through which the dancing could be seen, recognized, and re-cognized.

Cult of the Individual and the Appeal of Riverdance

Just as *Riverdance* seemed to a wide public to come out of nowhere, so did Michael Flatley. His self-aggrandizing approach to the theater and the media made him "good copy", that is, a personality very useful to the media interested in selling stories. And certainly one of the main stories that sells is the "one man" story, the individual who accomplishes the impossible against all odds, the hero, the individual behind an otherwise apparently social production: "I think, God bless Michael Flatley. His marketing technique, his ability to get publicity, good or bad, is keeping the whole show, him and Irish dancing, in the public eye" (Teacher, Limerick, 1999).

Michael Flatley must be given his due. He was intimately involved in the creation of two new genres of Irish dancing, the commercial-theatrical show (*Riverdance*) and the arena spectacle (*Lord of the Dance* and *Feet of Flames*). In addition to his dancing, his performing charisma and his ability to engage the popular press have brought continued attention to the form of dance that was his vehicle into the world of pop culture fame. His own image may swing from heroic to clownish in the media; however, by the principle that all publicity is good, Flatley's contribution to the place of Irish dancing on the world stage can hardly be questioned.

Ultimately, the question of whether Michael Flatley made Irish dancing or vice versa is moot. Irish dancing has made a performer of Flatley.

His creations, along with others, have helped bring world attention to Irish dancing. He may be a golden gloves boxer, a tap and flamenco dancer, but he is not known as a pugilist, tapper, nor bailaor. He is known as an extraordinary Irish dancer. It is this form of expression and its themes that have shaped him as a performer and that he has been able to exploit. Both made each other, just as Ireland's diaspora has helped to make Ireland, a principle of which Flatley is a token:

> He hasn't acknowledged his teachers. He said, like, he did it all for himself. You can't do anything for yourself unless you have the basis. . . . No matter how good Jean Butler and Michael Flatley were, that show would not have been as effective without the lines, lines of good dancers, excellent dancers (Teacher, Limerick, 1999).

In moving beyond fixation on Flatley, we can begin to see that some other ingredients were vital to the creative success of the production. Bill Whelan's continuing experiment in the fusion of Irish melodic sensitivity with Balkan and other East European rhythmic structures and phraseology played a crucial role in the dramatic success of the show. Jean Butler's dancing, grace, and stage presence cannot be overlooked, nor the impeccable dancing of the many Dublin area dancers who formed the corps that wowed audiences with their percussive precision. The whole production with virtuoso dancers, singers, and musicians under the productive direction of Moya Doherty made its mark as something new because all these people skillfully assembled forms, ideas, and impulses from so many tried and true expressive traditions.

When *Riverdance* exploded on the scene, it was the lines of dancers in precise time, thundering their rhythms, that people talked about. As much as Flatley has been able to amplify his claims to genius, the lines of Irish dancers coming on in waves, too many to give interviews, too similar in dress and style to be media individuals, made an unforgettable impression on audiences. In this way Irish dancing was the star of the show. The proof of this is the success of *Riverdance* after Flatley as well as the success of all the other shows that did not feature him. So while he has been instrumental in the media's recognition of Irish dancing, the dance form itself has made the world-wide impression.

This highly-developed technique du corps, dammed and developed through a century of competitive practice in the name of nationalism, burst upon the scene in *Riverdance* as a representation intact, a piece of Ireland. Even Irish audiences were amazed. *Riverdance* made Irish dancing "sexy," according to some Irish media critics, presumably because the costume was more flattering and the lead dancers moved their arms and turned their heads to make eye contact (MacDubhgail). There was a certain liberation in utilizing musical form which borrowed from Balkan time signatures. This was not the Irish dancing seen in the Gaelic League *Halla* or school hall down the road. The girls were not so little, were not wearing poodle-socks, nor hidden in costumes overloaded with Celtic kitsch in modern day-glo. *Riverdance* costumes accentuated the shapeliness of moving bodies without calling attention to themselves as galleries of icons. There were more equal numbers of young men and women on stage, suggesting mutual interest and participation. These features all marked *Riverdance* as different from the competitive form. But the movement itself, aside from the lead dancers, was precisely that of competitive Irish step-dancing, with slightly different musical phrase structure.

Indeed much of the power of the show and subsequent knock-offs lies in the great numbers of dancers in tight formations displaying a rigid discipline while thundering clever rhythms in unison stepping. They demonstrate a hyperbole of discipline, of self and group control, aggressive and threatening in the way that military drill foregrounds a power above the mere collection of individuals. The precision of the stepping and thus the power of the corps is obvious. Yet these are not gun-toting grunts but attractive young women and men dancing, playing with musical form and body rhythm. It is a peculiar mix of the sensual, musical, and martial.

Riverdance met with success based on an appeal that can be attributed to the impressiveness of the form and to its extraordinary display of discipline and expressive musicality. While these aspects of the form have been commonplace within the world of competitive step-dancing, their appearance in the theatrical and international context marks a new level of significance and signification for Irish dancing. The overt bodily discipline manifested in the carriage and the musicality of the feet are aesthetic transformations of deeper issues involving the morality and control of the expressive body that have been incorporated and developed through a history of changing political and economic realities.

One central theme running through this history is the ambiguous activity of dancing itself. Outlawed in Ireland by British authorities in penal times, dancing was vilified by various Church authorities in the last two centuries. At the same time, some forms of dance, those taught by dancing masters, were viewed as means of teaching manners and civility, a mission adopted by the Catholic Church in nineteenth-century Ireland (Inglis 1987:130-165). Finally, dancing was promoted as indigenous expression by the Gaelic League, but regularized in rules and standards of teaching and competitions. And in the Fianna Fáil blend of Catholic and nationalist authority, Irish dancing itself was held up as a model of morality in dancing. In the 1990s as the Catholic Church began to lose its place of traditional authority in Ireland,[8] even its preferred dance form could be made sexy and dangerous, as far as it went. But the rebellion against authority in dancing predates *Riverdance*. It is built into the very form of the dance.

Dance in Ireland, since the eighteenth century, has managed to survive by accommodating authority in the incorporation of restrictions (or, as in the case of social dancing, by avoiding the gaze of authority altogether and dancing at the crossroads). The resulting form of step-dancing embodies conflicting ideals, one might say, but works them out in a unique, Irish way. What is the Irish aspect of this solution? Perhaps it is the acceptance of the contradiction, the rejection of neither authority nor independent action but their juxtaposition, mutual incorporation, and elaboration in symbolic form. Thus the top half of the Irish dancing body betokens an overt discipline actually developed through competition, though linked conceptually and historically with impositions of the Church and the British Army. The lower half of the body meanwhile is the focus of individual creativity and expression, the distinguishing locus of performative authority.

It is not, however, only an Irish audience that can appreciate the combination of themes, values, images, and ideals expressed in *Riverdance*. The history of the body and expressive movement in Ireland is a particular version of a more general Western history of manners (Elias 1978). To some extent, anyone who has been told to "stand up straight" by one authority or another may be able to appreciate a form which incorporates that command while pulling off clever comments with the feet. "Be still" and "be quiet" are applied to the top half of the body, but loud or subtle, flamboyant and aggressive, or graceful movements are accomplished below.

Changes and Continuity

Riverdance adds a layer of rebellion within the Irish step-dancing world by not only taking its product outside competitive performance but also by making its product outside Irish dancing structures of authority. It is true that others in the world of Irish dancing have made theatrical shows previously, from aforementioned cabaret shows and folk festival performances to small theatrical tours. But these have by and large been productions of dancing schools, that is to say, almost a by-product of schools organized around the competitive institution. By utilizing dancers trained in the competitive world, but organized, rehearsed, and produced in the world of professional theater, the new shows move away again from An Coimisiún and such authority structures and thus answer to different standards of authenticity and institutions of control.

In this new context, Irish dancing has become a market commodity beyond the control of An Coimisiún. For example, recently one could find Irish dancing taught at an American college in a physical education or dance program by someone who does not hold a T.C.R.G.. While this was always possible, the popularity of Irish dancing resulting from *Riverdance* has created the actual demand. The changed landscape in which Irish dancing is now a recognized form raises some interesting questions regarding its continued development and the relations between its various settings of practice.

As the form moves from contests to touring theatrical shows, one might also argue that it has moved from one set of competitive rules to another, from a model of the competitive economy (the game) to the real thing. The market, of course, adds new and different evaluative measures of authority and authenticity; the bottom line begins to play an increasing role. However, still another course of development is also possible, that is, experiment with non-commercial theatrical settings. This is not an entirely new prospect. Siamsa Tire (National Folk Theatre, located in Tralee, Co. Kerry), the Trinity Dancers (Chicago, Illinois), and Patricia Mulholland's Irish Ballet (Belfast) are examples of groups that have experimented with blending Irish dancing and other theatrical genres with a claim to "high art" status. *Riverdance* created none of these initiatives but may have developed an audience for them. Even in the commercial shows, the producers' and choreographers' theatrical argument is that Irish dancing, while remaining in fact a national representation, is capable—like other "high" art or pop art—of universal significance. The success of the theatrical shows points to important ways in which Irish dancers have been able to escape the narrower world of nationalist representation and assert themselves as a transnational theater, drama and spectacle.[9]

The theatrical argument of *Riverdance* is that Irish dancing need not be so narrowly defined, and that it takes its place on a world stage as much through similarities and borrowings as it does through differences and distinctions. In that sense it is a timely message particularly in Europe where the construction of political unity in cultural diversity was and is a current and potent theme. It is significant, then, that *Riverdance* originated at the Eurovision song contest. To feature Irish dancing in a European celebration of music is already a claim of membership in a larger social context than the nation, yet one in which the nation remains important. If the lines of dancers performing straight Irish dance movement indicate the older symbol of the national dance, then the solo performers' blending, imitating, and playing with other forms creates the theatrical link to the larger, transnational context.[10]

There are two ways in which other forms were blended into the show. The full-length *Riverdance* show utilized Spanish flamenco dancers, Russian folk dancers, and American tap dancers to indicate the international context into which Irish dancing was being theatrically placed and featured. This creates an indexical link through simple proximity. But a further iconic link is established through imitation of other forms. In the original *Riverdance* production this was accomplished by Flatley's ability to execute some flamenco movement and dance with Maria Pagés in a Spanish piece. He was also able to incorporate both American tap and Flamenco footwork into his solo dancing. In later productions, scenes of Irish and African-American tap dancers imitating each other brought out similarities and differences in a sometimes humorous manner, also reflecting the informally competitive nature of solo step-dancing. The very fact that dances and dancers representing other nationalities, other peoples, other cultures appeared in a production featuring Irish dancing made the point of similarity and difference within the context of inclusiveness. This has had a reciprocal effect of changing the sense of Irish dancing as a symbol of nationalism.

Riverdance and *Lord of the Dance* include movement innovations that break the grammatical rules, so to speak, of Irish dancing and self-consciously challenge some defining limitations of the form. However, they do so tentatively. Arms, hips, and heads move, torsos twist, bodies touch, not just hands. However, this is true mostly for the lead dancers. The corps de ballet remains mostly well within the competitive form. Exceptions are hands being placed on hips instead of by the side. Small variations are woven into the largely standard variety of competitive step-dancing.

To make wholesale changes would risk losing the power of the form, its embedded history, upon which these productions rely for their impact. The competitive practice of Irish dancing and all the issues of paradox in national identity and change powered by competition are thus embedded in the new theatrical forms. In many other ways *Riverdance* has changed the symbolic nature of Irish dancing by changing the context in which it is seen, viewed, recognized, and evaluated. While the form and the literally contested meaning of Irishness in movement is still honed within the now traditional restrictions of the feis, a larger world of creation, experiment, presentation, and contest (including contested meaning) awaits the trained dancer.

The new theatrical productions featuring Irish dancing are thus adaptations of traditional and ongoing issues involving identity and change to new social, political, and economic worlds of relevance, including an emerging European State. I would argue that these themes are present everywhere to one degree or another in body movement practice of any culture. Irish dancers have simply made a game and an institution of these issues for over a century now. Powered by the engine of competition, they have developed the art of their technique du corps to astounding levels, apparent in shows like *Riverdance* and *Lord of the Dance.* Embedded in this artful movement are both old and recent questions and issues of how body movement signifies and what it means to be Irish in body movement. Meanwhile, to audiences outside the world of these contests, the form is as it must be, incontestably *Irish* dancing.

Theoretical Background and Analysis of Form

TABLE OF CONTENTS

To access the Appendix, please go to the following web address: http://supplemental.macaterpress.com

Notes

Introduction

[1] Later I get the welcome news that Michael won. Maybe his win redeemed Maureen's week. Years later I learn that Michael is dancing with *Lord of the Dance,* and then I see Rachael Ann again, at the World Championships. She no longer competes. She is a fan of the dancing, a supporter of the school.

I begin this study with a narrative to locate myself as an observer, an outsider, dependent on the goodwill of friends and consultants, and involved in a network of social relations, attitudes, and emotions. I would want to deny none of this. However, this study for the most part leaves this experiential dimension behind as a matter of focus and concentrates much more on Irish dancing as a form and practice of collective representation.

[2] "[A]bout it being Irish dancing as a [representation] of Ireland—I think it's an occupation of a very select group of families. And people of Ireland, mainstream Ireland, would probably know very little about it" (Galway dancer, 1991). In 1991, before *Riverdance,* many of my consultants considered the activity to be a very closed world with little appeal to the general public. And yet it was called Irish dancing. The popularity of the form, which ebbs and flows, is less an issue in this study than the internal issues raised by its claims of representation welded to the practice of competition.

[3] Terms of argument in authenticity can range from aesthetic effectiveness, market share, promotional presence, performer pedigree, and theatrical rhetoric, to historical preservation or folkloric integrity.

[4] Arensberg and Kimball, in *The Irish Countryman* and *Family and Community in Ireland,* defined an anthropological approach in the 1930s called the "community study." Their work represents some of the first ethnographies to be conducted in a European setting. (I refer here to ethnography in the Malinowskian tradition of mainstream anthropology—long term, theory-driven, participant-observation.) Shifting from the study of groups defined by tribal affiliations to the European setting, one methodological problem was to establish boundaries to their study. They chose to study a rural community of location, i.e., a town or village. This entity appears to be some sort of "natural" social grouping and made sense from the standpoint of social geography.

The community study became the dominant model for anthropological investigation in Ireland because it made methodological sense. Anthropologists using location-based studies have explored any number of topics from politics and mental health to farming and storytelling. Irish dancing could indeed be studied on this basis as well, and perhaps it will be at some not too distant time. The focus and fields of relevance would then relate more significantly to the community of location, its social, political, and economic relations.

In choosing an activity-based community, my focus and field of relevance have been placed more centrally on the networks of Irish dancing participants and the activity itself. It is not any better or worse in general, only better for some considerations and not for others. It is better for looking at some of the inherent connections between nationalist ideology and competitive practice and their combined effects on this expressive form and practice that have been institutionalized on a national and international level.

[5] This is the only ethnographic study of which I am aware that specifically addresses Irish negotiations of Irishness itself, a collective representation as a social process. It so happens that my work dovetails with a need, expressed by anthropologists at a conference on

"The State of Social Science Research in Ireland:"

"No extensive analysis, on the symbolic level, has been made of Irish culture(s). Local community studies, focusing on social organisation, have attempted 'holistic' pictures of the structural integration of communities, but these cannot provide a broad interpretive analysis of Irish culture(s). Within this context, the concepts of 'Irishness' and Irish identity, and their place in a cultural understanding of the island, are particularly in need of research" (Kane101-102).

[6] The constructedness of the term, "Irish dancing," including the exclusion of other dance forms is the subject of Chapter Two.

[7] As we will see, the term "modern" with respect to competition refers to competitions that are rationalized with institutions of control, codified rules, authenticated officials, and so forth. There are contests in sean-nós dancing, but as of yet there is no "Sean-nós Dancing Commission" or the like.

[8] I refer here specifically to the improvisatory form of sean-nós dancing. There is another form of old-style step-dancing, referred to as "traditional dance," which is based on choreographed steps created and passed on from the dancing master tradition. This variant is closer to the modern solo step-dancing tradition in the manner in which it is learned (classes), performed (symmetry in beginning each sequence first on the right and then repeating the sequence starting on the left, or vice versa), and in certain aspects of body use (posture tends to be more erect).

[9] The sets are tied (historically) to specific regions in Ireland, e.g., The North Kerry Polka, The South Galway Reel Set, etc. Locally they may have just been known as "the polka set" or "the set." However as the process of revival and popularization has taken these dances to wider audiences, the names tend to reflect their local affiliations. In one sense, these sets are not "Irish" because they do not claim to be anything more than local. On the other hand, they tend to share features across localities, features that are collectively different than quadrilles as they are danced in other locations like England, Canada, and the U.S. Thus in that respect they are Irish. For a full discussion of set dancing and locality, see Breathnach *Dancing*; Edwards; and Lynch.

[10] I am referring here to the use of a traveling step known in Irish dancing as the "threes," performed to four counts. This entails three changes of weight (on counts 1, 2, 3) and a rhythmic pause (on 4) per measure as opposed to the even two changes of weight per measure, as in a normal walking step. This step, as it applies to competitive step-dancing is explained in detail in Chapter Four. In contrast, the American version of the quadrilles—square dancing—utilizes a walking step (two even changes of weight per measure).

Chapter One

[1] Crossing the feet refers to foot placement mainly in steps but also in gestures, where the feet (and knees) should be placed one in front of the other rather than side-by-side, in a sagittal relation rather than horizontal.

[2] The process of adjudication is, of course, more complicated than the selection of single features. This is discussed more fully in Chapter 6 where creativity and change in the form are the central topics.

[3] Conradh na Gaeilge, The Gaelic League, was founded in 1893 as an organization dedicated to the revival and promotion of indigenous Irish cultural forms, especially language but also music and dancing. The important role of this institution in the development of Irish dancing is addressed in the next chapter.

[4] Cullinane, in *Aspects of the History of Irish Dancing*, includes a chapter based on oral history of dancing masters from living memories. In these accounts, descriptions of exotic

dress and pretentious airs give way to descriptions of dancing prowess, status in the social scene resulting from dancing skill, and occasional reference to teaching authority.

[5] Most historical references to dancing masters indicate that it was a male occupation in the eighteenth and nineteenth centuries.

[6] "Hegemony," in the sense that Gramsci used the word, i.e., as ideological power, describes the social and economic dominance of one group over another by means of which the dominated accept their place. Manners at once symbolize and are held to justify an arrangement of dominance and subordination through purported "natural" signs such as body use. Of course, they are also understood to be cultural to some extent, i.e., learned, and so the dominated can accept that learning manners is part of social ascendance, part of the learning they must do.

[7] The contradiction between manners and authentic social awareness is also woven into the conflicting interests of a person such as William Carleton who lives and moves between two worlds, unequal in many ways. Carleton was the son of Gaelic-speaking Catholic peasants, but he converted to Protestantism. He was one of the first successful authors with this type of background, i.e., Gaelic-speaking and Catholic, to write in the English language. He wrote for an audience composed largely of the Protestant ascendancy.

[8] The contradiction between aristocratic and republican ideals in the diffusion of manners in the American context is discussed at length in Bushman. I have not found a similar discussion in the Irish context, though I believe parallels are not far fetched.

[9] See Breathnach "Church and Dancing"; and various Bishops' "Lenten Pastorals" which appear in *The Irish Independent* through the 1930s, 40s, and 50s (e.g., 03 March 1930; 16 February 1931; 17 February 1958; and 16 February 1959).

Chapter Two

[1] This chapter does not attempt to address contemporary theoretical debates on topics of nationalism, transnationalism, and globalization. While there is much that could be explored here, the present description and argument is limited to the historical development of Irish nationalist cultural organizations and the roles that two of these (Gaelic League and Irish Dancing Commission) were able to play in shaping the identity and practice of stepdancing in the twentieth century.

[2] This period is also referred to as the Irish Ireland movement, the cultural nationalist movement or revival of Irish culture. See Boyce 237-42; Garvin, *Nationalist Revolutionaries* 78-86; and Lyons, *Culture and Anarchy* 57-83. One can also trace the intellectual thought of this movement back to earlier times, e.g., the writings of Thomas Davis in the 1840s (Cronin 67-71; Lyons, *Ireland Since* 224). However, as a popular movement, the founding of the G.A.A. remains a useful marker of commencement.

[3] The case of literature is, perhaps, the most well-known with the controversies surrounding Hyde, Synge, Yeats, Lady Gregory and the status and direction of the Anglo Irish literary renaissance (See Lyons, *Ireland Since* 233-46; *Culture and Anarchy* 57-84; and Kiberd passim).

[4] Fréine, *The Great Silence* 108 (qtd. in Kiberd 151). Kiberd goes on to discuss the double appropriation of the kilt—the Irish from the Scots, and the Scots from an English Quaker industrialist "*after* the highland clearances" (ibid., emphasis in original).

[5] The politicization of cultural forms was both a matter of applying nationalist ideology to existing genres of expressive activity of the native population, and also a matter of inventing forms to fill the niches created by the rejection of valued English cultural possessions.

[6] The problems of written descriptions of movement are brought out with respect to Irish dancing by Cullinane, *Aspects of History* 6-10. In a larger theoretical context they are

discussed by Williams, *Ten Lectures* 86-87.

[7] As explained in the Appendix, description of the formal structure of cultural forms depends in part on native (dancers' and teachers') conceptions of units and levels. This implies further problems for historical movement study.

[8] Some problems with the argument are: 1.) the equation of musical forms with dance forms represented by the same linguistic tag; and 2.) the assumption that the jig is Irish, which begs the question being asked. This last assumption is reflected in the certainty that the English didn't invent it, thus taking current cultural identifications as proof of origins.

[9] The term *céilí* translates as "friendly call; visit; social evening; Irish dancing session; dance" (*Foclóir Póca* 299). The last two of these meanings are the direct result of Gaelic League usage. This usage originated with an event sponsored by the Gaelic League of London. This event and additional etymological information is described in Carolan 8-9; and Cullinane, *Aspects of History* 16-17.

[10] Carolan traces the dances (which appear in O'Keefe and O'Brien through the collecting work of the London chapter of the Gaelic League) back to Kerry dancing masters who modeled these dances on quadrilles. He uses the Gaelic League's documentary sources to explain the pivotal role of Professor P. D. Reidy who was engaged by the London group to teach dancing. Reidy had been a dancing master in Ireland and was the son of a Kerry dancing master. According to Carolan, Reidy himself attributed the creation of the céilí dances to an instruction given to the dancing masters by the Knight of Glin at the end of the Napoleonic Wars to produce group dances on the quadrille model (9).

Carolan traces the relation of sets and céilí dancing to the modeling of one form on the other, though with independent authorship under the authority or encouragement of an historical Irish figure, the Knight of Glin, referred to by Reidy. This is a more specific version of a process Cullinane theorizes in which dancing masters would not have necessarily required the instruction from the Knight of Glin to, in effect, re-create group dances.

[11] Cullinane's data for his argument regarding the common origins but different development of set and céilí dancing are the memories of various informants, oral histories, and documents, as well as the formal similarities and differences between the two forms of dancing. Three features of this analysis stand out: 1.) that he does not rely on arguments about origins which lie beyond the purview of the scholar working in non-literate, ephemeral forms; 2.) that he recognizes the aspect of physical education (discipline) in the step-dance form as taught by dancing masters and suggests that the dancing masters introduced some of this discipline into the social dance forms; and 3.) that he accounts for the formal differences in terms of elaboration and points to the role of the dancing masters who had motivation for elaborating the form more than peasants dancing strictly for pleasure.

[12] Of course another layer of politics is also institutionalized in the struggle for control over such national institutions. In Irish dancing, as in other institutions, the struggle includes the geographic/social/economic dimension of the center versus periphery, Dublin and the rest of Ireland, as well as the diaspora. This dimension of institutional politics is beyond the scope of this work, with the exception of breakaway organizations described in the next section.

[13] Contemporary representation of the Gaelic League on the Irish Dancing Commission is closer to one in five, and most often these are positions are held by dancing teachers, adjudicators, or close relatives to dancing participants.

[14] The second tension (center-periphery) has not led to a formal organizational split, though it may always be a source of complaint. The Irish Dancing commission eventually set up its own provincial councils, and eventually district councils for England, North America, and Australia as well. Other dance teachers' organizations still exist, though are not necessarily seen as threats to the Dublin center of the Commission.

[15] Nationalist ideology does not require continued and radical adherence to either/or

logic. Mulholland's practice is a case in point. Her interpretation of Irishness was inclusive.

Chapter Three

[1] Although I applied for permission to attend meetings of An Coimisiún, it was not granted. Various reasons were given, but they all shared the common thread that An Coimisiún was a closed group and did not want to set the precedent of allowing non-members to attend. Therefore I was unable to witness the actual conduct of business. I talked with nine commission members, three of whom were former Presidents at different times, conducting interviews with four of them. I also reviewed the minutes of several An Coimisiún meetings during the 1930s, 40s, and 50s with the help of a translator, as minutes from these meetings were written in Irish. Currently, Commission business is conducted in English; however, I was unable to gain access to minutes from more recent meetings.

[2] At the time of this writing a solo dancing dress can easily cost €600-1000 ($900-1500).

[3] The evaluative aspect of any performance genre makes possible its adaptation to the agonistic model of events. Two fundamental assumptions generate the modern model of aesthetic competition: 1.) that dance performances can be compared; and 2.) that the performances can be arranged in a hierarchical order. The adjudicator is then in the role of rationalizing his/her results to meet requirements of the assumption. This rationalization of the aesthetic leads to other implications, for example, that winning form can be taught and learned, as in the case of Catriona's desire to be told what she needs to do to win.

[4] The case of movement innovation is more specifically addressed in Chapter Five.

[5] My own sense, and it can only be an impression, from having watched numerous competitions, is that the judging is mostly very fair. Occasionally one sees results that look as if a competitor has been unfairly graded down. However, the biggest fault would more likely be overly conservative judging, where last year's prize-winner earns first-place votes more on her reputation than on her actual performance on the day. Some people would defend this approach to judging, much as is done in boxing, where the victory has to be decisive to unseat the champion. It could just as easily be seen as conservative nature of adjudicators more worried about agreeing with each other than venturing "an honest opinion." At any rate, it would appear that this conservative approach fits in with the pressures of competition as analyzed here.

[6] An older point system ranked first at 12 points, second at 5 points, and third at 2 points. "Our system is based on the theory that two second placings should not equal or exceed in points value one first placing, nor two third placings equal or exceed in points value one second placing. It is interesting to note that our system has been very favourably commented upon for its logic and fairness by people and groups unconnected with Irish dancing" (MacConuladh, *Finding Winners* 7).

[7] The interpretive approach to games has been pioneered in cultural anthropology by Clifford Geertz. The crucial abstracted elements of Geertz's (449-50) formulation of the cockfight are: 1.) the fact that the rules of the game are in all cases selections of thematic concerns from the culture and society playing it; and 2.) that the ongoing object of the game beyond winning and losing is the use of emotion for cognitive ends in the understanding of the inner relations of these selected thematic concerns.

Chapter Four

[1] I would argue that the relationship of movement to speech is that of a continuum. There are movement systems, such as sign languages, that are very much like spoken languages, with lexicon, tense, aspect, and many other features of spoken language, including grammar and syntax. And there are movement systems that are much less discursive. However, since humans are talkers, it is ultimately impossible to separate the way movement

means from the way other aspects of culture mean, including spoken language. This is not to deny that dance and movement in general gain some rhetorical power or other effect by being a modality other than speech.

[2] I estimate contemporary participation on the beginning level of Irish dancing to be in the neighborhood of 85% female. According to the official list of the Irish Dancing Commission for 1991, in Ireland there were 75 female adjudicators and 32 male adjudicators (70% female); there were 247 female teachers and 45 male teachers (85% female) (*Liosta Oifigiúil*).

[3] Indented italicized text, where not specifically referenced, is synthesized from field-notes, mostly with the Hession School of Dance in Galway, 1991. Photographs are from 1991 and 2008. The descriptions of the teacher and school in this chapter are based on a composite of six teachers in three schools in Dublin, Limerick, and Galway. Not all schools of Irish dancing may fit the following description. The names used are fictitious.

[4] Sometimes these relationships continue across generations; e.g., a woman may take her daughter to the same dance school she attended as a child, where the same teacher or another from her family is to be found.

[5] Jigs are in 6/8 meter, slip jigs in 9/8, reels in 4/4, hornpipes in 2/4. For definitions of dances and their meter, see Ní Bhriain. For a classic discussion of Irish dance music see Breathnach (*Folk Music* 55-64).

[6] Competitive dancers can often be seen at competitions reviewing the sequence of a dance using their feet as they are seated in a chair, or using their hands on their laps as if they were the feet, or even using the first two fingers of a hand on the pad of the thumb to simulate the feet. Mnemonic devices are thus not strictly or only verbal, especially for competitive level dancers. However, the verbal modality never seems to go away either, as a mnemonic and descriptive device.

[7] I would like to thank Miki Bird for suggesting this comparison.

[8] For a technical description of the movement analysis of formal structure that informs this chapter, see the Appendix.

[9] See Williams's article (1995) on Tai Chi Chuan, the ballet Checkmate, and the Latin High Mass as movement systems illustrating three different systems of relevant spatial coordinates.

[10] The importance of rhythm and tone of speech to spoken language can be briefly summarized in the comment, "It ain't what you say but the way that you say it" (See Crystal 69-173). The meaning of a spoken (we might say enacted) utterance can be highly dependent on these features. The close relationship between speech, music, and movement in terms of "what one is saying" should militate for an expanded notion of language that does not refer to words alone, but takes into account tone, movement, and other features of the human organization of material life. Equally implied in this point of view, the study of human movement should not be radically separated from the study of speech and music. Many of the same principles are at operation in each of these modalities. In this regard see, Farnell 293-303, and passim; and Williams *Ten Lectures* 178-207.

[11] My use of the term "style" is non-technical in the sense that it is not theoretically tied to usages such as those found in Royce (*Anthropology* 157-158); or Kroeber passim. As the title suggests, I use the term to refer in various contexts to how movements are performed. In this context, the beginning class, there is a normative sense to "style", i.e., a proper way to perform the movements. In other contexts, dancers, teachers and adjudicators may speak of an individual's style, which is not a matter of norms, but distinctions.

[12] A turn-out originating in the ankles may appear to be an anatomical impossibility as the ankle is normally considered a hinge joint with only the actions of flexion and extension possible. However, articulations between the tarsal joints permit inversion and eversion as

well as a certain amount of sliding side to side (Gray 285-289). Thus it is possible for an Irish dancer to effect a slight turn out of the foot while keeping the knee oriented forward in the sagittal plane. This is not to argue that Irish dancers never turn out at the hip; rather, this is kept to a minimum: a flattened eversion of the foot achieves a degree of turn out while keeping the knees more closely aligned with the sagittal plane.

[13] "Extension" here means keeping the foot in line with the lower leg along the longitudinal axis. This is known in anatomical/medical terms as plantar flexion of the foot; however, dancers often recognize it as "extension" of the foot. "Extension," as used here, means the same for all leg parts, i.e., lining up the parts along the longitudinal axis with the next highest (proximal) limb section.

[14] The horizontal dimension is neutralized or eliminated, as it were. There is no obvious preference for right or left in the form, with the possible exception that steps may begin with the right foot forward, weight on the left. In a sense, the right leg is being presented as in former notions of bowing etiquette. But all steps in competitions have to be danced beginning on the right foot and then repeated beginning on the left foot, once again bringing about a right/left symmetry.

[15] The difference between aesthetic competitions and other sports that do not center on the aesthetic element, is the centrality of evaluation. A purposive sport is one in which, within the rules or conventions, there is an indefinite variety of ways of achieving the end (and largely defines the game). By contrast, an aesthetic sport is one in which the purpose cannot be specified independently of the manner of achieving it. For instance, it would make no sense to suggest to a figure skater that it did not matter *how* he performed his movements, as long as he achieved the purpose of the sport, since that purpose inevitably *concerns* the manner of performance (Best 104-105).

As Bauman has pointed out, the performance situation is defined by two elements: 1.) a framing device, i.e., some device for calling attention to the expressive act for 2.) special consideration of *the manner* in which the act is carried out. While performance is a mode of communication that is emergent from mundane communicative practices, the example of Irish dancing demonstrates the performance frame at a logical extreme. The frame is a contest of proclaimed representation of national identity in danced movement. The frame is keyed by such devices as stages, costumes, music, and the special system of movement itself. While in the beginner's class they work solely on the movement, the larger context of competition informs the process (9-11).

Chapter Five

[1] Creativity may be more or less expected in a dance form, depending on its own history, traditions, and relations to other socio-cultural forms. Modern dance, for example, is a genre that celebrates creativity far more than tradition—even its name signals this value. Irish dancing involves both creativity and tradition sometimes in a dynamic relation of antithesis, the subject of this chapter.

[2] It may seem that freedom and restriction should be at odds in dancing, but they are interdependent as with all art forms. Without the effect of restrictions, the freedom to create is meaningless and ineffective; there would be no "form" only random movements. Without certain regularities in the formal features of a particular movement genre, we would not be able to recognize it as a genre.

[3] This distinction is only a convention because reordering existing units at one level always produces new units at another level. However, there are inventions, often at very low levels of structure in the movement system, which are recognized as introductions to the system, i.e., new movements, even when these can be analyzed as another sort of reordering of movement bits. This is precisely what happened with "the butterfly," analyzed below.

[4] I have chosen the slip jig, a light dance, i.e., performed in soft shoes in 9/8 time, for ease of analysis. With a soft shoe dance it is possible to demonstrate important competitive elaborations without subjecting readers to intricate analysis of audible rhythmic stepping in addition to movement in space and time. Both dances come from the Hession School of Dance, Galway in 1991. The champion's dance was Gemma Carney's at age 15.

[5] Technical terminology has mostly been avoided in the chapter text. What are here called "moves" would be kinesemes, technically. See Appendix for more detailed explanation of the ordering and structuring of movements at different levels of analysis.

[6] The mythology of this practice, however, may owe more to vaudeville than the country kitchen, where half-doors, hollow flags, and even plates were said to provide dancing surface. A recent account reports "*Oireachtas* title-holder, Máirtín Mac Dannacha of Ráth Chairn, whose parents originally came from Connemara, for want of a plate, occasionally dances on a dartboard!" (Brennan 138). One is reminded of Flann O'Brien's description of the poverty in Corkadoragha. Are the poor residents of Ráth Chairn forced to eat off the dartboards as well?

[7] Names of steps are not consistent. Often steps are imitated and named without any personal or pedagogical contact between the performer and imitator. "Toe stand" is a name used by some and the step would probably be recognized by that name among most teachers, dancers, and adjudicators.

[8] I am told by a teacher that "Many contemporary champion Irish dancers would have at some point taken ballet or gymnastic classes." This certainly illustrates the nearness of ballet as potential influence. But it would not necessarily be the case that ballet students introduced the toe stand. It is a perfectly logical extension of the aesthetics and techniques of Irish dancing. In either case, the toe stand could not possibly exist without the semantic link to ballet, because of its familiarity.

[9] One recent innovation, of which I am aware, is a metal reinforcement built in to the light shoes which help a dancer maintain an arch in the feet, for better pointing of the toe and dancing "up on the toe."

[10] This name was given to it by its creator, Marie Duffy. There are, however, other movements that are referred to by other dancers as "butterfly." There are also other names given to the movement described here as the butterfly. Ultimately the movement can only be known by its execution or representation in notation. As a matter of interest, in 2008 I was told that the butterfly went out of fashion some ten years before.

[11] Some critics of the butterfly claimed it came from ballet, though I have reviewed the step with ballet dancers who were as intrigued with its character as anyone. It does not come from ballet, although there is a slight similarity to ballet steps known as *entrechat quatre* and *entrechat six*.

[12] Indeed, this pattern of change is recognizable in the ballet that began as social dancing in the court of Louis XIV and developed into a specialized form of theater. But even here we can find matters of distinction and training in bodily expression claiming an early importance. It is partly in complement with the courtly notion of distinction that the rural peasantry is given its image of simplicity.

Chapter Six

[1] *Riverdance* was originally performed as an interval entertainment at the annual European song contest, Eurovision. It is a very popular event televised throughout Europe and several other parts of the world. The country sponsoring the winning act hosts the following year's event and provides entertainment while the judges calculate scores and decide the winner of the contest. Ireland hosted in 1994.

[2] The Gaelic League in 1929 appointed Coimisiún na Rinnce (Commission on Dance)

to look into and make recommendations with respect to problems in the dancing competitions. This body became *An Coimisiún le Rincí Gaelacha* (The Irish Dancing Commission) in 1930. See Chapter Two. While Brennan; and Cullinane, *Aspects of History,* et al., have each addressed aspects of this historical change, little work on the particulars of these discussions, debates, and changes has been done to date.

[3] The equivalent game of hurling for girls is called camogie. It is the same game; however girls play camogie and boys play hurling. There are no mixed games.

[4] This is not to say there had been no theatrical versions of Irish dancing. In America Irish dancers could be found in Vaudeville and later, for example, by a young Michael Flatley at the Indiana Fiddlers Gathering in the mid-70s or in tours of Comhaltas Ceoltoiri Eireann and The Chieftains. In Ireland, Irish dancing was a part of variety concerts throughout much of the century before television changed habits of entertainment, and even into the nineties continued to play a small role at fundraising concerts, variety shows, or tourist cabarets.

[5] In addition it is calculated that some eighteen billion people have watched *Riverdance* on television. These figures are from the Riverdance.com website.

[6] Two interesting developments in American clogging circles have been: 1.) the inclusion of "Riverdancing" in performances by cloggers, i.e., dancers trained in American step-dance rather than Irish dance technique, but imitating what they see on videos of *Riverdance* and other Irish dancing shows; and 2.) the production of whole shows along the Riverdance model, even referred to as, for example, "America's Response to Riverdance" (in Jamison).

7 The question of where the Worlds Championships are held continues that ongoing process of reckoning with the international constituency of Irish dancing. In 2002 for the first time the World Championships were held outside of the 32 Counties, in Scotland. And in 2009, also for the first time, it is being held in the United States.

[8] Journalist Fintan O'Toole, among others, has addressed some of the causes for this loss of moral and political authority ("Mixed Blessings").

[9] Transnational is a word and concept with far from precise meaning. I use the term here to approach the developing relations of significance when a "national symbol" is used to make claims to supranational or extranational identities. It is nothing new. In some ways, the celebration of St. Patrick's Day by many ethnicities and nationalities in America is a good example. *Riverdance* is the example *par excellence* of this phenomenon, especially because the dancing which it featured came from a narrow and exclusionary nationalist setting.

[10] There is also a slippage of meaning that accompanies this move to the international world of theater and spectacle. Irish songs, musical forms, myths, and legends are easily appropriated, commodified, and re-contextualized for easy consumption. It is not so much a problem for the dancing as it has already been stripped of many local resonances by the competitive process. In a self-conscious attempt to capitalize on the already successful commercialization of "Celticism," these dance shows commodify expressions—a sean-nós song here, a slow air there—to give the spectacle its dramatic flow and keep it easily digestible by audiences that do not know or care to know the relationship between the expressions and the people from whom it came. This is a trade-off irksome to some (O'Toole, "Unsuitables") but to be expected in the move to global spectacle.

Works Cited

Anderson, Benedict. 1983. *Imagined Communities: Reflections on the Origin and Spread of Nationalism.* New York: Verso, 1993.

Ardener, Edwin. "Introduction to Social Anthropology and Language." Ardener: *The Voice of Prophecy and Other Essays.* Ed. M. Chapman. Oxford: Blackwell, 1989. 45-64.

—. "The New Anthropology and its Critics." *Man* 6.3 (1989): 449-67.

—. "Some Outstanding Problems in the Analysis of Events." Edwin Ardener: *The Voice of Prophecy and Other Essays.* Ed. M. Chapman. Oxford: Blackwell, 1989. 86-104.

Arensberg, Conrad. *The Irish Countryman.* 1937. New York: Natural History, 1968.

Arensberg, Conrad, and Solon T. Kimball. *Family and community in Ireland.* Gloucester, Mass.: Smith, 1961.

Ar Rinncidhe Foirne. Dublin: An Coimisiún, 1939.

Bauman, Richard. V*erbal Art as Performance.* Chicago: Waveland, 1977.

Bauman, Richard, and Joel Sherzer, Joel, eds. *Explorations in the Ethnography of Speaking.* Cambridge: Cambridge UP, 1974.

Best, David. *Philosophy and Human Movement.* London: Allen, 1978.

Birdwhistell, Ray L. Kinesics and Context: *Essays on Body Motion Communication.* Philadelphia: U of Pennsylvania P, 1970.

Bourdieu, Pierre. *The Logic of Practice.* Trans. R. Nice. Stanford: Stanford UP, 1990.

Boyce, D. George. *Nationalism in Ireland.* London: Routledge, 1991.

Bushman, Richard L. *The Refinement of America.* New York: Knopf 1992.

Breathnach, Brendan. "The Church and Dancing in Ireland." *Céim* 47 (1978): 3-4.

—. *Folk Music and Dances of Ireland.* Dublin: Mercier, 1971.

—. *Dancing in Ireland.* Milltown Malbay: Dal gCais, 1983.

Brennan, Helen. 1999. *The Story of Irish Dance.* Dingle: Brandon.

Brown, Lesley, ed. *The New Shorter Oxford English Dictionary on Historical Principles.* Oxford: Clarendon, 1993.

Carleton, William. "Buckramback, The Country Dancing Master." *Tales and Sketches of the Irish Peasantry.* Dublin: Duffy, 1845. 15-29.

Carolan, Nicholas. "The Beginnings of Céilí Dancing: London in the 1890s." *Céim* 69 (1990): 8-9.

Carty, Peggy. *My Irish Dance.* Galway: Carty, 1987.

"céilí." *Foclóir Póca: English-Irish/Irish-English Dictionary.* Dublin: An Gúm, 1986.

Charteris, J., and P. A. Scott. "Structuring the Domain of Human Non-verbal Behavior: A Biological, Popperian Perspective from the Field of Human Movement Studies." *Semiotica* 95.3/4 (1993): 205-234.

Comerford, R.V. "Nation, Nationalism and the Irish Language." *Perspectives on Irish Nationalism.* Eds. T. Hachey and L. McCaffrey. Lexington: UP of Kentucky, 1989. 20-41.

Corkery, Daniel. *The Hidden Ireland: A Study of Gaelic Munster in the Eighteenth Century.* Dublin: Gill, 1956.

Cronin, Seán. *Irish Nationalism: A History of its Roots and Ideology.* Dublin: Academy, 1980.

Crystal, David. T*he Cambridge Encyclopedia of Language.* Cambridge: Cambridge UP, 1987.

Cullinane, John, ed. *Aspects of the History of Irish Dancing.* Cork: Cullinane, 1987.

—. *Further Aspects of the History of Irish Dancing.* Cork: Cullinane, 1990.

—. *Aspects of the History of Irish Dancing in North America.* Cork: Cullinane, 1991.

Edwards, Bridget. "Making the Floor Talk: Irish Social Dance as Cultural Juncture." Diss. Indiana U, 2000.

Elam, Keir. *The Semiotics of Theatre and Drama.* London: Methuen, 1980.

Elias, Norbert. *The Civilizing Process.* 2 vols. New York: Pantheon, 1982.

Farnell, Brenda. "Plains Indian Sign-talk: Action and Discourse among the Nakota (Assiniboine) People of Montana." Diss. Indiana U, 1990.

Fine, Elizabeth C. *The Folklore Text: From Performance to Print.* Bloomington: Indiana UP, 1984.

Fraleigh, Sondra H. *Dance and the Lived Body.* Pittsburgh: U of Pittsburgh P, 1987.

Franken, Marjorie A. Review Article. *Journal for the Anthropological Study of Human Movement* 8.1 (1994): 65-70.

Fréine, Sean de. *The Great Silence.* Dublin: Foilseachain Náisiúnta, 1966.

Gabor, Robert. "Origins of the Feis in Ireland." *Aspects of the History of Irish Dancing.* Ed. John Cullinane. Cork: Cullinane, 1987. N. pag.

Garvin, Tom. *The Evolution of Irish Nationalist Politics.* New York: Holmes, 1981.

—. *Nationalist Revolutionaries in Ireland, 1858-1928.* Oxford: Clarendon, 1987.

Geertz, Clifford. "Deep Play: Notes on the Balinese Cockfight." *The Interpretation of Cultures.* New York: Basic, 1973. 412-453.

Gell, Alfred. "On Dance Structures: A Reply to Williams." *Journal of Human Movement Studies* 5 (1979): 18-31.

Glassie, Henry. *All Silver and No Brass.* Bloomington: Indiana UP, 1975.

—. *Passing the Time in Ballymenone.* Philadelphia: U of Pennsylvania P, 1982.

Goffman, Erving. *Presentation of Self in Everyday Life.* New York: Doubleday, 1959.

Gramsci, Antonio. *Prison Notebooks.* New York: Columbia UP, 1992.

Gray, Henry. *Anatomy: Descriptive and Surgical.* Rev. New York: Bounty, 1977.

Hall, Edward. *The Hidden Dimension.* New York: Doubleday, 1966.

—. *The Silent Language.* New York: Doubleday, 1959.

Hall, Frank. "Improvisation and Fixed Composition in Clogging." *Journal for the Anthropological Study of Human Movement* 3.4 (1985): 200-217.

—. "Posture in Irish Dancing." *Journal for the Anthropological Study of Human Movement* 8.2 (1994): 251-266.

Handler, Richard. *Nationalism and the Politics of Culture in Quebec.* Madison: U of Wisconsin P, 1988.

Hastrup, Kirsten. "Fieldwork Among Friends: Ethnographic Exchange Within the Northern Civilization." *Anthropology at Home.* Ed. A. Jackson. London: Tavistock, 1987. 94-108.

Henry, Edward O. "Institutions for the Promotion of Indigenous Music: The Case for Ireland's Comhaltas Ceoltoiri Eireann." *Ethnomusicology* 33.1 (1989) :67-95.

Herzfeld, Michael. *Ours Once More: Folklore, Ideology, and the Making of Modern Greece.* Austin: U of Texas P, 1982.

Hobsbawm, Eric. Introduction. *The Invention of Tradition.* Eds. Eric. Hobsbawm and Terence Ranger. Cambridge: Cambridge UP, 1983. 1-14.

Holdcroft, David. *Saussure: Signs, System, and Arbitrariness.* Cambridge: Cambridge UP, 1991.

Hutchinson, Ann. *Labanotation.* New York: Theatre Arts, 1977.

Hutton, A. W., ed. 1892. *Arthur Young's Tour in Ireland in the years 1776, 1777, and 1778.* 2 vols. London: Bell, 1892.

Hymes, Dell. "The Ethnography of Speaking." *Anthropology and Human Behavior.* Eds. T. Gladwin and W.C. Sturtevant. Washington: Anthropological Society, 1962. 13-53.

Inglis, Tom. *Moral Monopoly: The Catholic Church in Modern Irish Society.* Dublin: Gill, 1987.

Jaeger, C. Stephen. *The Origins of Courtliness: Civilizing Trends and the Formation of Courtly Ideals, 939-1210.* Philadelphia: U of Pennsylvania P, 1985.

Jakobson, Roman. "The Dominant." *Readings in Russian Poetics: Formalist and Structuralist Views.* Eds. L. Matejka, L. and K. Pomorska K. Cambridge: MIT P, 1971. N. pag.

Jamison, Phil. "Mountain Legacy: A Celebration of Southern Appalachian Dance and Music." *The Old-Time Herald* 6.3 (1998): 12-14.

Judy, Jo Ann. 1989. "Ann Richens: A Modern Irish Dancing Master." *Dance Teacher* 11.8 (1989): 14-20.

Kaeppler, Adrienne. "Cultural Analysis, Linguistic Analogies and the Study of Dance in Anthropological Perspective." *Detroit Monograpahs on Musicology: Explorations in Ethnomusicology* 9 (1986): 24-33.

—. "Method and Theory in Analyzing Dance Structure with an Analysis of Tongan Dance." *Ethnomusicology.* 16.2 (1972): 173-217.

—. *Poetry in Motion: Studies of Tongan Dance.* Tonga: Vava'u, 1993.

Kane, Eileen, et. al. "A Review of Anthropological Research in Ireland, North and South." *The State of Social Science Research in Ireland.* Ed. L. O'Dowd. Dublin: Royal Irish Academy, 1988. 95-110

Kealiinohomoku, Joann. "An Anthropologist Looks at Ballet as a Form of Ethnic Dance." *Impulse* (1969-1970).

Kiberd, Declan. *Inventing Ireland: The Literature of the Modern Nation.* London: Vintage, 1996.

Kroeber, Alfred. *Style and Civilizations.* Berkeley: U of California P, 1963.

Lakoff, George, and Mark Johnson. *Metaphors We Live By.* Chicago: U of Chicago P, 1980.

Leonard, Hugh. "The Unimportance of Being Irish." *Irishness in a Changing Society.* New York: Barnes, 1988. 18-29.

Levi-Strauss, Claude. *The Savage Mind.* Chicago: U of Chicago P, 1966.

Liosta Oifigiúil Na Moltóirí Cláraithe agus Na Múinteóirí Cláraithe. Átha Cliath: An Coimisiún, 1991.

Lynch, Larry. *Set Dances of Ireland: Tradition and Evolution.* Milltown Malbay: Dal gCais, 1989.

Lyons, F. 1979. *Culture and Anarchy in Ireland, 1890-1939.* Oxford: Clarendon, 1979.

—. 1971. *Ireland Since the Famine.* London: Fontana, 1971.

MacAodha, Breandán. "Was this a Social Revolution?: The Gaelic League and Other National Movements." T*he Gaelic League Idea.* Ed. S. O'Tuama. Dublin: Mercier, 1972. 20-30.

MacConuladh, Seamus. "An Coimisiún le Rincí Gaelacha—What Is It?" Dublin: *An Coimisiún,* 1987.

—. "Finding the Winners: The Point System." *Céim* 8 (1972): 7-9.

—."Origin of An Coimisiún Le Rincí Gaelacha." *Aspects of the History of Irish Dancing.* Ed. J. Cullinane. Cork: Cullinane, 1980. 1-2.

MacDubhail, Uinsionn. "Putting the Sex Back into Irish Dancing." *The Irish Times* 05 May 1994.

Mandle, W. F. "The Gaelic Athletic Association and Popular Culture, 1884-1924." *Irish Culture and Nationalism, 1750-1950.* Eds. O. MacDonagh, W. Mandle, and P. Travers. New York: St. Martin's, 1983. 104-121.

—."Games People Played: Cricket and Football in England and Victoria In the Late Nineteenth Century." *Historical Studies* 15 (1973): 511-35.

—. "The I.R.B. and the Beginnings of the Gaelic Athletic Association." *Irish Historical Studies* 20 (1977): 418-438.

—. "Sport as Politics: The Gaelic Athletic Association 1884-1916." *Sport in History: The Making of Modern Sporting History.* Eds. R. Cashman and M. McKernan. Brisbane: U of Queensland P, 1979. 99-123.

Mauss, Marcel. "Body Techniques." *Sociology and Psychology Essays.* London: Routledge, 1979. 95-123.

McCourt, Frank. *Angela's Ashes.* New York: Scribner, 1996.

Messenger, John C. *Inis Beag Revisited.* Salem, Wis.: Sheffield, 1983.

Ness, Sally Ann. *Body, Movement and Culture: Kinesthetic and Visual Sym-*

bolism in a Philippine Community. Philadelphia: U of Pennsylvania P, 1992.

Ní Bhriain, Orfhlaith. *The Terminology of Irish Dance.* Madison: Macater, 2008.

Nic Shim-Uí Dhálaigh, Eilis. 1985. "A Very Big Question—What Can Be Done?" *Céim* 53 (1985): 13-14.

Nowlan, Kevin B. "The Gaelic League and Other National Movements." *The Gaelic League Idea.* Ed. S. O'Tuama. Dublin: Mercier, 1972. 41-51.

Noyes, Gertrude. *Bibliography of Courtesy and Conduct Books in Seventeenth Century England.* New Haven: Tuttle, 1937.

O'Brien, Flann. 1941. "The Dance Halls." *Bell* 1.5 (1941): 11-52.

O'Keefe, J.G., and A. O'Brien, A. *A Handbook of Irish Dances.* Dublin: O'Donoghue, 1902.

O'Rafferty, Peadar, and O'Rafferty, Gerald. 1953. *Dances of Ireland.* London: Max Parrish and Co.

O'Toole, Fintan. "Mixed Blessings. Annie and the Bishop, Ireland and America." *The Lie of the Land: Irish Identities.* London: Verso, 1997.

—. 1997a. "Unsuitables From a Distance: The Politics of Riverdance." *The Ex-Isle of Erin: Images of Ireland.* Dublin: New Island, 1997.

Page, Joann. "A Comparative Study of Two Movement Writing Systems: Laban and Benesh Notations." Diss. University of Sydney, 1990.

Peace, Adrian. "From Arcadia to Anomie: Critical Notes on the Constitution of Irish Society as an Anthropological Object." *Critique of Anthropology* 9.1 (1989): 89-111.

The Polite Academy: or, School of Behaviour for Young Gentlemen and Ladies. London: Baldwin, 1768.

Poole, Roger. "Objective Sign and Subjective Meaning." *The Body as a Medium of Expression.* Eds. J. Bentham and T. Polhemus. 74-104. London: Allen, 1975. 74-104.

Puirséal, Pádraig. *The G.A.A. In Its Time.* Dublin: Purcell, 1982.

Reisman, Karl. "Contrapuntal Conversations in an Antiguan Village." *The Ethnography of Speaking.* Eds. R. Bauman and J. Sherzer. Cambridge: Cambridge UP, 1989. 110-124.

Rialacha. Átha Cliath: An Coimisiún, 1991.

Royce, Anya P. *The Anthropology of Dance.* Bloomington: Indiana UP, 1977.

—.*Movement and Meaning: Creativity and Interpretation in Ballet and Mime.* Bloomington: Indiana UP, 1984.

Saussure, Ferdinand. *Course in General Linguistics.* New York: McGraw, 1966.

Seeger, Tony. Class lecture. Bloomington: Indiana University, 1987.

Sheehan, J.J. *A Guide to Irish Dancing.* London: Denver, 1902.

Small, Jackie. Interview with Brendan Breathnach. *The Dance Music of Ireland.* RTE Radio. Dublin. 1991.

—.Interview with Joe O'Donovan. *The Dance Music of Ireland.* RTE Radio. Dublin, 1990.

Spencer, Paul, ed. *Society and the Dance.* Cambridge: Cambridge UP, 1985.

Sturtevant, William C. "Studies in Ethnoscience." *Theory in Anthropology: A Sourcebook.* Eds. R. Manners and D. Kaplan. New York: Aldine, 1968. 475-500.

Taylor, Lawrence. "*Bás InÉirinn:* Cultural Constructions of Death in Ireland." *Anthropological Quarterly* 62.4 (1989): 175-87.

—. "The Healing Mass: Fields and Regimes of Irish Catholicism." Archives de Sciences Sociales des Religions 71(July-September 1990): 93-111.

—."The Mission: An Anthropological View of an Irish Religious Occasion." *Ireland from Below.* Eds. Curtin and Wilson. Galway: Galway UP, 1989. 1-22.

—. "Stories of Power, Powerful Stories: The Drunken Priest in Donegal." *Religious Orthodoxy and Popular Faith in European Society.* Ed. E. Baldone Princeton: Princeton UP, 1990. 163-181.

Turnbull, Colin M. *The Mbuti Pygmies: Change and Adaptation.* New York: Holt, 1983.

Varenne, Hervé. 1989. "A Confusion of Signs: The Semiosis of Anthropological Ireland." *Semiotics, Self and Society.* Eds. B. Lee and G. Urban. NY: Mouton, 1989. 121-152.

—.1993. "The Question of European Nationalism." *Cultural Change and the New Europe: Perspectives on the European Community.* Eds. T. M. Wilson and M.E. Smith. Boulder: Westview, 1993.

Veyne, Paul. *Did the Greeks Believe in Their Myths?*: An Essay on the Constitutive Imagination. Chicago: Chicago UP, 1988.

Wilkinson, Desmond. "'Celtitude,' Professionalism, and the Fest Noz in Traditional Music in Brittany." *Celtic Modern: Music at the Global*

Fringe. Eds. M. Stokes and P. Bohlman. Metuchen: Scarecrow, 2003. 219-256.

Williams, Drid. "On Structures of Human Movement: A Reply to Gell." *Journal of Human Movement Studies* 6.4 (1980): 303-322.

—."Prefigurements of Art: A Reply to Sebeok." *Journal for the Anthropological Study of Human Movement* 4.2 (1986): 68-90.

—.The Role of Movement in Selected Symbolic Systems. Diss. Oxford University, 1975.

—."Semasiology: A Semantic Anthropologist's View of Human Movements and Actions." *Semantic Anthropology.* Ed. D. Parkin. London: Academic, 1982. 161-181.

—."Taxonomies of the Body, with Special Reference to the Ballet, part 1." *Journal for the Anthropological Study of Human Movement* 1.1 (1980): 1-19.

—."Taxonomies of the Body, with Special Reference to the Ballet, part 2." *Journal for the Anthropological Study of Human Movement* 1.2 (1980): 98-122.

—.*Ten lectures on Theories of the Dance.* Metuchen: Scarecrow, 1991.

Wilson, Thomas M. "From Clare to the Common Market: Perspectives in Irish Ethnography." *Anthropological Quarterly* 57.1 (1984): 1-15.

Wulff, Helena. "Reverberations of Riverdance: Irishness, Technology and the Global Marketplace." Unpublished paper. 1999.

Wycherley, W. *The Gentleman-Dancing Master.* London: Herringman, 1673.

Young, Arthur. *A Tour in Ireland 1776-1779.* 1892. Dublin: Irish Universities P, 1970.

Index